TAROT

THE DIDACTIC TAROT

"BE. DO. THINK. FEEL. CHANGE."

JEFFREY M. DONATO

4880 Lower Valley Road • Atglen, PA 19310

Copyright © 2015 by Jeffrey M. Donato

Library of Congress Control Number: 2015930496

All rights reserved. No part of this work may be reproduced or used in any form or by any means—graphic, electronic, or mechanical, including photocopying or information storage and retrieval systems—without written permission from the publisher.

The scanning, uploading, and distribution of this book or any part thereof via the Internet or via any other means without the permission of the publisher is illegal and punishable by law. Please purchase only authorized editions and do not participate in or encourage the electronic piracy of copyrighted materials. "Schiffer," "Schiffer Publishing, Ltd. & Design," and the "Design of pen and inkwell" are registered trademarks of Schiffer Publishing, Ltd.

Type set in Beekman/Bodoni MT/Helvetica Neue LT Pro/Minion Pro

ISBN: 978-0-7643-4940-9
Printed in China

Published by Schiffer Publishing, Ltd.
4880 Lower Valley Road
Atglen, PA 19310
Phone: (610) 593-1777; Fax: (610) 593-2002
E-mail: Info@schifferbooks.com

For our complete selection of fine books on this and related subjects, please visit our website at www.schifferbooks.com. You may also write for a free catalog.

This book may be purchased from the publisher. Please try your bookstore first.

We are always looking for people to write books on new and related subjects. If you have an idea for a book, please contact us at proposals@schifferbooks.com.

Schiffer Publishing's titles are available at special discounts for bulk purchases for sales promotions or premiums. Special editions, including personalized covers, corporate imprints, and excerpts can be created in large quantities for special needs. For more information, contact the publisher.

I respectfully and lovingly dedicate this creation to:
my mother Pamela who nurtured me,
my father Jeffrey who taught me,
my sister Amy who believed in me,
my brother Joshua who created with me,
and to my beloved Raven,
who has loved me perfectly
and whom I adore.

  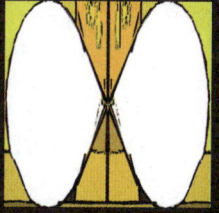

"This may very well be my revelation!"
—Fledgling

CONTENTS

Foreword: by Roxi Sim 6

Preface 8

Introduction 9

Chapter 1: *Con Vitalis:* The Great Book of Life 13

Chapter 2: The Fable of Fire: "BE" 23

Chapter 3: The Epic of Earth: "DO" 41

Chapter 4: The Anecdote of Air: "THINK" 59

Chapter 5: The Words of Water: "FEEL" 77

Chapter 6: The Diffusion: "PAUSE" 101

Chapter 7: The Tale of Time: "CHANGE" 115

Usage 150

Bibliography 160

FOREWORD
—Roxi Sim

What an honor to be asked to write the foreword for Jeffrey's new deck, *Tarot D: The Didactic Tarot*. What an interesting title. According to one reference:

> Didacticism is a philosophy that emphasizes instructional and informative qualities in literature and other types of art. The term has its origin in the Ancient Greek word (didaktikos), related to education and teaching, and signified learning in a fascinating and intriguing manner.

Since this deck was created for Jeffrey's Master's degree in Fine Arts thesis, and his goal is to teach the Tarot through symbolism, it is an apt title.

I met Jeffrey through the Tarot Deck Creator's page on Facebook, which I created together with Pamela Steele of *Steele Wizard Tarot* and Bonnie Cehovet, author of *Tarot, Birth Cards, and You: Keys to Empowering Yourself*.

We asked artists to post their Tarot images and write-ups to share with other artists. It was a great way to bring together kindred spirits and artists painting the same theme of the Tarot. When I first saw Jeffrey's very detailed images I was thrilled. The cards were bright, busy, and full of symbolism, much like my *Pearls of Wisdom Tarot* deck. I knew instantly that Jeffrey and I drew from the same creative well. I love his rich colors, artistic style, the sense of depth he has created, and the emotion his work evokes.

In keeping with the teaching nature of his deck, Jeffrey generously allowed Pamela and me to use his images, as well as his intensive artistic process, to share in our "Tarot Deck Creation" webinar series through Global Spiritual Studies. For his Master's thesis, Jeffrey had documented his progression through each card from drawing to underpainting, coloring, and inking. He also showed how he achieved consistency through the suits with color and theme.

Jeffrey's deck will be one to ponder, study, and meditate upon. Some images will fill you with whimsy, others perhaps even horror as, you know, Tarot covers all aspects of life. An original approach to the Tarot, *Tarot D* has so much to offer. The busy images ensure that new things will pop out each time you see a card. Though it may take a little more time to read and comprehend than other decks, you certainly will never be bored. It was wonderful to hear that an artist from our Deck Creators Page and group was to be published. Our goal is to widen the audience of Tarot and push the boundaries at the same time. Jeffrey's deck does both with flying colors. Congratulations Jeffrey!

Roxi Sim (Hermsen) Dip. Fine Arts, B. Ed. Fine Arts, 5th year Art and Dance therapy. Roxi is an internationally acclaimed artist. Her art is in collections in Europe, the Caribbean, and North America. Her Tarot deck is a favorite in collections around the world. Soon to be an app, *The Pearls of Wisdom Tarot*, also has an upcoming workbook/journal.

PREFACE

On the subjects of art and Tarot, I would be remiss if I didn't confess: oftentimes I feel that they are like an expressive dream, the unconscious language of the soul. Only you can interpret what they mean to you. Sometimes it's a blatantly obvious "slice of life," other times it's completely cryptic, and the abstract symbols dare you to try to make sense of them. Dreams, just like art and Tarot, can be erotic, frightening, and even prophetic. After we've experienced a dream and we awaken to reality, we feel something...deep down. It stays with us and becomes a part of us forever. If we try to discuss it with others afterwards, there's always a disconnection. Something is lost in the translation. We may have shared in the same dream experience, but our individual perceptions, born out of our life experiences, are what construct the dream itself. Were we even looking at the same piece of art or the same spread of cards? No, we weren't— just like we didn't have the same dream. There's nothing definitive about it. It's a big, nebulous cloud of brain candy. Go ahead and have a piece! Every symbolic illustration I've created for this Tarot deck is designed to be an extraction from the dream we all share, as well as an expression of my relationship with art. However, it is up to you to decide what it really means to you!

I have dubbed this work of mine *The Didactic Tarot*, because the process of creating it has been exactly that. I was a novice before and I can only claim to be slightly more than that now. Life is learning, and acceptance of this fact is the greatest gift one can ever give to oneself. It appreciates failure as part of the process and rewards questions with answers that lead to even deeper questions. I am hopeful that as it has engaged my desire to learn and cultivate a clearer perception of the Tarot, and life in general, that my *Didactic Tarot* will somehow awaken that desire in others.

INTRODUCTION

The book you now hold is the key to unlocking the secrets of the universe! Well, okay—maybe not. But the illustrations that accompany this book may very well be just that. I was advised by someone (with significantly more knowledge on the subject than I, who, perhaps as a ritual at this point, generally throws the "little white book" accompanying any new Tarot deck away as soon as he's opened the box), that if I were to write my own book about the Tarot, I should approach it from an "artist's point of view." Seeing as how I am, first and foremost, a storyteller and visual artist, I suppose this would be inevitable. However, to suspend all other considerations because of laziness, poor research, or simply for the sake of slaking my own thirst for lucid entertainment would be counterproductive to the ultimate goal I have set for myself.

In the following pages I will introduce you to my imagined universe and its hierarchy. The story will be a tale of the first gods and how they created all life. Space, Time, Energy, and Matter are the primary forces that bring everything into focus. From there, the five-fold aspects of existence come into play: Being, Doing, Thinking, Feeling, and Changing. Each one of these modes of existence corresponds to an elemental suit. Fire is the essence of Being, Earth is the foundation of Doing, Air is the substance of Thinking, Water is the element of Feeling, and Time is the genesis of Change. This is the theme and mantra of my Tarot. This is how I use the elements and their symbolism to define the patterns and cycles of life. By looking at these five concepts and how they operate in synchronicity with one another, we might get a truer sense of what it means to be human.

Reproduction is a recurrent theme throughout the *Tarot D*, hence the obvious, gender binary represented throughout the pip cards. Each pip card has a male and female symbol to show that it is not a complete idea until both aspects are present. Despite this being a theme, the Tarot encompasses ideas that, while traditionally given a specifically masculine or feminine association, transcend identity, gender, and sexuality.

The Dynastic Chinese "cardinal compass points" place particular significance on North, East, South, and West as being elemental as well as seasonal strongholds. Since this is where I first found inspiration to study symbolic correlations to the elements cross-culturally, I paid special attention to include this in my deck. My "diffusion" suit is completely derived from this concept. I switched the East and West elemental positions. This being the case, in my *Didactic Tarot,* North is Water, East is Air, South is Fire, and West is Earth. The Master is seated to the left and the Keeper to the right of the elemental direction. The Bearers are bound towards the opposite direction of their element, and the Acolytes are pursuing the Bearers in search of adventure in other lands. As far as relationships between the elements go, think of it as a balance of power. Fire is extinguished by water. Earth is scorched by fire. Air is displaced by earth, and water is at the mercy of air. The border of each card is color-coded by its elemental suit. Each also displays other symbols besides just numerals and western zodiac signs. There are planetary equivalents and moon phases as well. These are present to aid the reader in deepening the symbolic meaning.

This is my mountaintop—a foothill nestled within the shadows of the many more daunting peaks I have yet to conquer. I welcome you. Sit, and let me tell you my version of the tale. It's the great story, the one that we have all heard since before any of us were ever born and it is told by the eternal echo of the source and the void. I have chosen to present my *Didactic Tarot* as a myth through the words and voice of one who reads from an imagined, divine book that tells the great story. The following segue signifies my transformation into your narrator. Open your mind and suspend disbelief as I take you on a journey into the depths of my imagination. Enjoy! -D

"Art is my magic spell. My brush is the implement of consecration. Paint is the blood of my sacrament. My creative energy is the purifying fire. I am invoking divine power through this ritual of expression. I banish darkness and embrace light...the radiant light of the lamp of God."

—Reverend Isaac Sylvan (Aggregate of the Ecliptic)
The Eternal Continuum of Peace, Love, and Truth

...and so the story was made known to me, and I remembered all that I had forgotten.

CHAPTER 1

CONVITALIS

THE GREAT BOOK OF LIFE

That which now *is*, never was. Born and dying in the silence between the endless rows of cosmic lamps. Each of us is a star and a luminary unto the untold glory of Prion. That light, which guides us, is the sacred way inward. *Follow me!* in the footsteps of the God of gods and the mystery of thought that spirals like endlessly twisting, woven ladders, and coils of Matter and Energy into the very pit of the atoms that make us Be. Like the Serpent and Her shadow, from the farthest star into the nearest, shining heart we will travel. Each of us is a five-pointed sigil and a gateway into the depths of the primordial oceans that, by and through transcending, we might find and hatch the collective egg from which emerged Energy and Matter… the soundless sound, the breath and voice of Prion.

How to explain the unexplainable? How to unravel the enigma that is? How to create for you a container within which to hold and carry these secrets of eternity? That which exceeds itself and is all things excluding none must be born by being unborn and thusly make what is unmade and bring what IS into being. A blink to the unmoved mover, Prion, is all that is, was, and will be. Space, as it was before Time, is every possibility and impossibility floating within an eternal moment, poised to be caused by Being. Doing seemed in error by the logic of Thinking, and in a subtle swell of Feeling, God Thought Doing Being Changed. Stretched to the unreasoned ending, in entropy the shadow of Prion's first and only action was revealed.

Divine spark, ignite!

Source and Void, each as limitless as the other, engulf and regenerate in perfect unison, until each overtakes the other. Prion could not unmake Himself. By Being to Do and by Thinking that Feeling could unmake that which was unmade everlasting instead became that which was and yet was not. She was awakened, and so perished Space without Time and henceforth persisted that which could never Be: Nema. As Prion became, so did Nema consume and contract into nothingness. The Source and the Void enraptured and entwined in the infinite. The totality was known and unknown to both. What was, is, and ever shall Be, as well as what is not and may never become. By Being, Prion had chosen not only to acknowledge His own existence, but also to act upon that existence in such a way as was purely instinctual and essential. This brought forth the first Doing. Prion began the great manifestation, calling into Being every moment of existence at once. It was in this eternal moment that Nema began to form. She was a shadow cast upon the universe as Prion emerged. She only had the power to devour and make things a part of Herself. In understanding His desire to act, Prion realized that by Doing, He could create. Those notions of creation would become the essence of all reality.

Nema could never devour as fast as Prion could create. The vast worlds of strange creatures that Prion made were violent and powerful. He took pleasure in creating creatures so strong that Nema could scarcely contend with them. But contend She did. She took many clever forms in order to do so. She eventually consumed them all and made them a part of Her. This was the essence of the first conflict originating in the separation of the wills. Prion recognized that Nema was His shadow and would no doubt have to be Thinking in much the same manner He Himself was. Light casts shadow and shadow devours light. The understanding of reason and remembering became the power to control the other. Prion Felt loneliness. He Felt purposeless. He desired the relief of nullity, of non-existence. But how can God cease to exist? Prion chose to destroy Himself. He chose to transform. Upon changing, Nema's will was born from His entropy.

Prion, the suicidal God, only succeeded in creating a Shadow of Himself.

Nema's very existence is Time in motion. She is a part of all that has become since Prion Himself became. She devoured Prion, for, as She is His shadow; She is compelled to Be all that He is. She must eat Prion. She must absorb all that He is to become all that is. Then all that is will Be all that is not. As Prion was compelled to expand, so Nema too was compelled to consume. And when Prion could stretch Himself no further, Nema devoured Him completely. All was unmade except for His eternal heart, which burned ever bright in the deepest depths of the void. When the limit of the limitlessness was devoured by shadow, the Un-being collapsed around His bright and burning heart and Being overflowed from its container… the very container you now carry a piece of. Then, Nema collapsed on Herself and Prion transformed a part of Her from inside. Their union became Primordea: the only pure element. It is the enigmatic plasma of the infinite. It is the Aethyr, called into the form of a dodecahedron, in all that can exist. Thus, the cosmic egg was lain and began to hatch. The most powerful part of each of their Beings had become fused into an infinitely dense sphere. Then, that sphere hatched, as an egg would, exploding with such a force that it shattered both Nema and Prion. He became the endlessness of Space. She became Time, seeping through the universe and slowly devouring all that She finds. The sphere, upon exploding, split in even symmetry and the two halves distinguished themselves as Matter and Energy. Interchangeable though they were, they chose these separate forms. That choice is the first dimension of Being according to Prion.

Spinning wildly through the vastness of Space, Matter, and Energy desperately tried to reunite, but to no avail. They left behind the universe in the wake of their spiraling dance. Every star and planet is a part of them, created by their repeated collision. He is Energy. She is Matter. Their names are Eon and Iode. Together they are the broken heart of the universe. Prion is their Father and Nema is their Mother. When they were born they were the will of Prion, and Nema was seemingly obliterated by their genesis. But soon, Nema began to re-coalesce. Her hunger was insatiable. She must devour Her children to reclaim eternity and make all nullity in Her likeness. Prion has become Space again and now lies dormant in the dimension outside of Time. Time is Nema. That which Prion created came into Being by not Being at all. When Prion stretched Himself to the unreasoned ending, He shattered and the shards of His essence established the five dimensions of existence: Being, Doing, Thinking, Feeling, and Changing. And so, all of the magic and divinity that Time and Space would ever know was pulled into one place and from there made to radiate outward in all directions. The shards of Prion overlapped and intertwined. By becoming these separate planes of existence, Prion made Himself into something that could Be reconstructed by the will of others. Eon and Iode began to collect their Father's pieces, and each one whispered secrets to them. If they were to bring all of the shards together and plant them in the fertile essence of their individual, yet cooperative wills, a crystal tree would grow. The tree would stand as an altar to Prion and a way to commune with Him, and thereby with every facet of existence. Eon and Iode then set upon the task of remaking what had been unmade by the temporal shadow. Ages of unrecorded Time passed and each shard that was found revealed ideas that would not be conceived of for ages to come.

Recollecting Herself, Nema began to reform, but She was weak and She knew Her own diminished power would not Be enough to regain control over the universe. She would have to rebuild Herself by reabsorbing the power of Prion, one shard at a time, and then She would grow powerful once more. She would have to turn that which was into that which could never again Be. Finally, after untold millennia, Eon and Iode planted the crystal tree from all the shards of Prion they had collected. The tree grew quickly and emanated magic of the deepest kind. The children of the universe then fell into a peaceful slumber, not aware that their Mother was approaching, intent on reabsorbing them into Her depthless womb. As they slept, the crystal tree was dismantled and the shards that the twin demiurges had used to build its

seed were scattered into four elemental dimensions. When they awoke, they found themselves bound to the tree's final remnants. Hence, Eon and Iode came to know fear. Their Mother had found them. Disguised as a slithering shadow, She'd crept up on them and wound Herself around the pulsating roots of the crystal tree, siphoning power from its perfect presence. She would use this stolen power to ensnare Her children and transform them into nothingness that She could then absorb. From Her manipulation of the most primeval of Prion's power, there came a SPARK! The essential seed that was used to plant the crystal tree burst forth flame. Nema sacrificed Her children to Herself through this, the first element: FIRE, believing that by using Prion's power against them, they would ultimately Be destroyed.

And so began the transcendent journey of Eon and Iode....

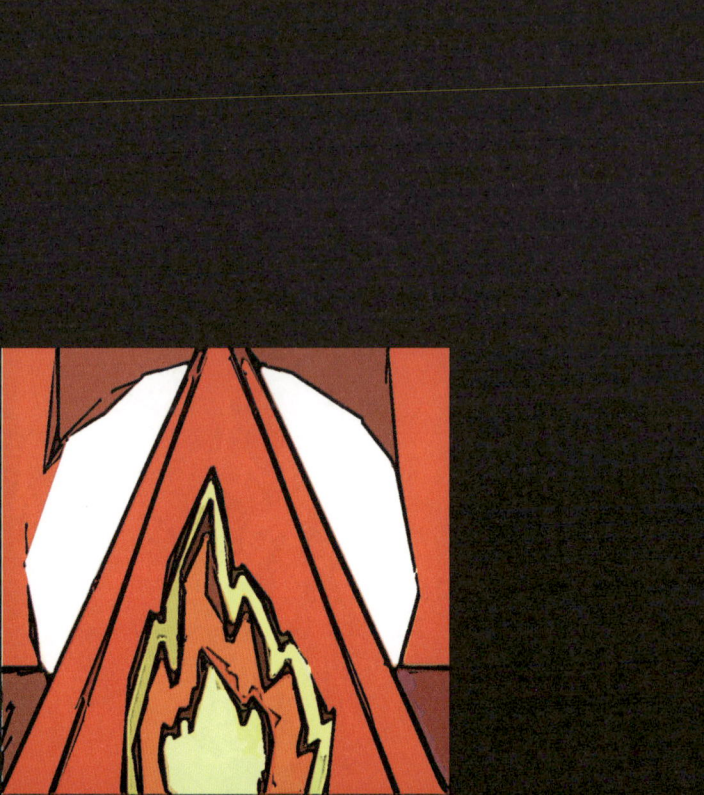

CHAPTER 2
THE FABLE OF FIRE
"BE"

REMNANT ASHES

Awake, Eon and Iode did, inflamed to burn as sacred pyre. From Shadow's light, the fearful scourge of Time had come to devour Her children.

We are the ancient seeds of the universe! We burn ourselves as a sacrifice to appease the supreme darkness, our Mother: Nema. We turn our bodies into ashes to feed Her depthless hunger. We purify our souls, now released from Her encircling shadow. There is nothing left of our secrets. We leave behind no trace. We pass through the elemental barrier, made perfect through the purification of primordial flame and become one with the spirit of perfect light, our Father: Prion, who slumbers.

Meaning/Stage: a rude awakening, despair, torturous loss of one's soul, loss of self

Reversal: an offering made to the gods, a rite of passage, purification through fire, pagan ritual, funeral pyre, first rung of the ladder

THE ALTAR TO THE ESSENCE OF FIRE
(ACE OF WANDS)

Their powerful essence was a perfect union of Prion and Nema. Through the passage they arrived and then became the fire of beings.

> With this seed of Prion we resurrect in the Temple of the Tetrahedron, the dimension of the perpetual flame. His scepter, his phallus, is the wand with which creation was ignited. It is the candle of existence from which all energy is drawn. It is the branch that falls not from a tree, clutching its igneous fruit: a metamorphic orb containing the ghosts of unborn gods. It is the key to the door that leads to the sun, through the core of the unmade planet: Terra. The essence of Being is what we've become…one eternal spirit.

Meaning/Stage: energetic, confident, engaged, eager to begin, creative force, enthusiasm, confidence, courage, new passion, new religion or career, energy augmentation, heat, desire for more, moving forward, ambition, growth, progress, gain, the magic wand

Reversal: lull, immobility, inertia, broken plans

BURNING QUESTIONS
(2 OF WANDS)

The power of the fire grew as they reclaimed the first shards of Prion. If the altar held more shards it would unlock the next dimension.

Mingling flames illuminate our pathway towards the radiant star. Though treacherous and fraught with shadows, we let our caprice guide us through. Decisions are made and steps are taken, forward, upwards, ever rising. We bring forth fire, Ammram's breath, stolen from his elliptical prison. What we seek impels us onward. Burning questions drive us forth. What will we find beyond this place, power, violence and Prion's embrace. Take us in your fiery hands and convey us towards your perfect plans.

Meaning/Stage: searching, prepared for new adventures, personal, power, boldness, originality, having to decide which passion to focus on, a choice- if made correctly that will reward your instincts, careful planning, system, extension of the self, determination

Reversal: stay alert and aware, do not overlook the finer details

DISPLAYS OF POWER
(3 OF WANDS)

Set on separate paths, hoping both would be successful; the power of their efforts was conceived to bring them something better.

A fervid mouth with tongues of lava spewed us forth from out its maw. Our kingdom now is lain before us, and all there is to be explored. Great reptilians roam the surface. Something lurks in the distant sky. It's fled to tell its Master Mother. Soon She will come and we cannot hide from Her. So let us be bold and step apart and see what each can become alone. Then we'll recombine and gain new strength. The horns of fire from which we drink and stoke our spirits make us strong and give us a sense that we belong. This is our realm and so we claim the power of the perfect flame.

Meaning/Stage: empowered, positive action, and movement, a time to grow and build upon strong ideas and impulses, exploration, foresight, leadership, progress, anxious to see if the investment of passion will pay off, a sense that you are on the brink of success, pride, impulsiveness

Reversal: deconstruct and start from scratch, retooling

SEASONS TURNING
(4 OF WANDS)

From the shards they claimed it, drawing forth the perfect power. They acquired the ability to BE and see and wish for something beyond themselves.

The land's spirit is forged by the fiery anger of the Great Ram. What begins like shallow breathing, bursts as a star and unleashes the fury of creations beasts. The Ram comes roaming and is not alone. Never to be tamed, it forges the core of the planet's contours with its horns and leaves the celestial orb's blood to pool with fragments of the star. So we draw it in and soak it up and make ourselves anew. A circle of fire that imbues us with the power of a god fallen from the sun. The history of what might be is shown to us, a wondrous sight to behold.

Meaning/Stage: excited, empowered, fulfilled, preparedness, a timely and useful answer, a blessing of sorts, celebration, freedom, arrival of ships, the belief system and empire have been established, foundation for the future, bask in the glory

Reversal: repelled, banishment, everything is taken away, expenditure

BREAKING BRANCHES
(5 OF WANDS)

Set upon by evil Shadow's paragons, they were! Eon did tear the virile heart from out the villain's chest while Iode lay scarred and wounded.

> The Lion's roar shakes the Earthly pillars and shatters the black calm, blanketing the forest of despair. Breaking loose from the cage of thorns, the fire makes ashes of the perpetual black. The poisoned power, its soul container, spewing bloody shadow, is absorbed as a spoil of war, and soon will taint the deepening darkness. This is the first of many wars we will engage in with the horde. The shards of Prion give us strength to kill the shadows on the brink and scorch the deadly, jagged wood, purging it of evil until it regrows green, just as it should.

Meaning/Stage: a feeling that the world is against you, fighting back, disagreement, competition, excitement, power struggles, conflict, confusion, panic, inner doubts, leaping into the fray and doing battle, hard work

Reversal: collective efforts, cooperation creates success

TRIUMPHANT RETURNS
(6 OF WANDS)

He brought her home. They both received new power after their ordeal. The world was pure and grateful. Now it was time to BE and oversee.

The Great Lion strides across the planet leaving meadows in its paw prints, watering flowers with its breath, and all life bows before it. Tumultuous sounds of birds and horns and trumpeting creatures profess their love. The path is strewn with fronds of palm, cherry blossoms and rose petals. Victorious and glorious we, the children of the universe, celebrate and now remake that which has been in ruin. This is our kingdom, a welcome home. Enjoy this time. Be free and roam. Spread the love that's been collected, give it back to those who you've protected.

Meaning/Stage: relieved, happy, cheerful, accomplished, a moment in the sun, but do not be haughty lest you be played the fool, some may be jealous of your strength, triumph, acclaim, pride, victory, a solution was found, return from battle with the spoils and an answer, you are the hero, success

Reversal: a time for respite, relaxation, vacation

THE UPPER HAND
(7 OF WANDS)

And so, they stood above the shadows. The advantage belonged to them for now. The perfect essence gave them both the strength of endless legions.

> The Nemites would count coup on us before striking down our weak defenses. Laughing bold and loud, they pointed low, but now our roles are reversed. We stand above the brittle horde and let them taste our fiery words. A mere glance from a burning stare will wipe them away in one swift stroke. As the lion shakes its mane the shadows are engulfed in flame. We reclaim the thrones that are not yet built and watch the blackness scream and melt away as power does remake the home of Prion. Now none may enter and not be burned. The shadows flee. A lesson's learned.

Meaning/Stage: willful power, righteous indignation, vengeance, its time to stand up for yourself and show your power, aggression, defiance, conviction, under attack from all sides, under siege, on the defensive, you have the high ground—but you must defend yourself relentlessly

Reversal: keep your power a secret, don't reveal yourself until the last possible moment—then your enemies won't have time to prepare a defense, internal conflict

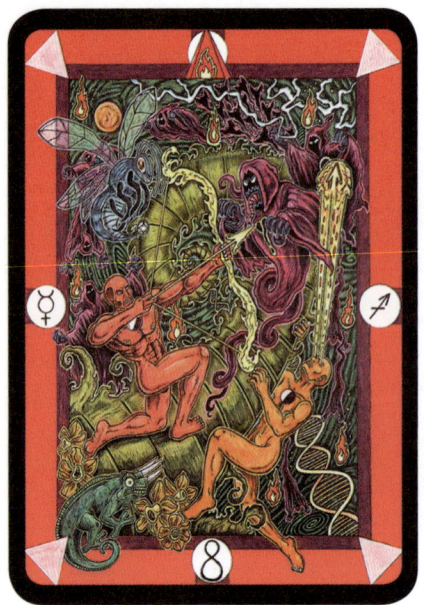

SWIFT OCCURRENCES
(8 OF WANDS)

They climbed the spiral towards the moon, with arrow swiftness, killing doom, proceeding deep into the void to alleviate Nema's grasp.

An arrow flies from out the sun, golden power of the Father sent to penetrate the darkness and to shed His perfect light. The legions will attack us but the power doth repel them to their Mother's deep and deadly womb beyond the corona. Atop the endless spiral we are racing to confront Her and to supplant Her in Her throne of death that circles now and watches. Renewed our strength and with fresh resolve, stirring anger in our bellies full of fireflies, we take to the sky to face the one who comes to devour us.

Meaning/Stage: inspiration, an urge to attack, impelled forward, take charge, take the battle to them, quick action, conclusion, news, movement, expansion, chasing the retreating horde to their lair and killing them all along the way, control, show 'em who's boss! travel may be suggested as well as Cupid's arrows of love

Reversal: someone might be manipulating and luring you into a trap, danger ahead, over-enthusiasm

POISED AND READY
(9 OF WANDS)

Shattered shards of star were released by an arrow shot straight through her center. The satellite called Luna regained her presence of mind. Her countenance returned to normal. Eon and Iode were merely marred by the battle. Still prepared to fight, they retreated to where the power would be regrown.

> Her sphere of death is a floating orb without a soul, come to absorb the life from all that live and breathe. The moon, it has become Her throne of nightmarish dreams. Twilight will arrive and She will roam across the sky and change the world. Her designs will now be thwarted by an arrow piercing through Her void. Her heart, or lack thereof, is filled with fire and bursts, emancipating a billion captured stars. And so She goes to sleep, and others will be tasked with keeping Her throne a place of nocturnal peace.

Meaning/Stage: wounded by weathering the storm, a scar heals over twice as strong, cautiously attend to your wounds, get ready for round three, defensiveness, perseverance, stamina, climbing a seemingly endless staircase, exhausted but still prepared for battle, its time for the final push, use those reserves of energy to attain the highest goal…it is within sight, integrity

Reversal: surround yourself with those who you trust to help you in the coming battle

HEAVY BURDENS
(10 OF WANDS)

From the reformed seed of fire, regrew the crystal tree. The tree protected the altar and the core became a new beginning. Too much for only one to carry, it had to be given some release.

The sequence of the ladder is built from branches of the crystal tree. Now its crown of glowing leaves is transformed into tongues of flame. The power, far too much to hold, is formed into orbs of Prion's essence. Each orb will collect the elements and become a regeneration of Prion. These guiding orbs will help in times when the burden of leadership becomes too great, so that those who follow can consult with God Himself to gain insight. The truth that comes with enlightenment is an understanding of this mortal coil. A trap it Be for the spirit, once free, now sequestered and imprisoned until death liberates it.

Meaning/Stage: weary, exhausted yet still carrying on, accountable, lots of work, shouldering the responsibilities of many, overextending, burdens, struggle, you are the boss, you've accomplished and won, but now the burden of leadership is yours, you must delegate responsibility because you have used up all of your elemental power dealing with the weight of primordial fire, recharge your spiritual and libidinous energy

Reversal: slothful neglect, things are falling apart, time to stabilize, restriction

THE FORTRESS OF FIRE
(THE ROARING INFERNO)

With the power of ten shards the key was formed. They erected the fiery fortress. This was where the demigods would rule and ancient myths would find beginnings.

> The Ram will sit enthroned beside the Lion and the Archer. The Salamander and the Phoenix will raise the child of fire to be the first Alchemist and guardian of the sacred power of spirit. Upon erecting the fortress in the dimension of the flame, we gain new powers and understanding. We become one with the essence of the element that Nema will try to control but can never become, for this is the purest element wherein all life first begins. The core of the Earth itself is a roiling ball of molten fire around which the body of our planet wraps itself. The fire within generates all the essence of life that will be propagated upon the planet. It is the forge of spirit.

Meaning/Stage: home of the spirit, a place of spiritual awareness where you are at one with your true self

Reversal: A place of deception where there is no clarity and lies are swirling

THE ACOLYTE OF FIRE
(PAGE OF WANDS)

The Acolyte was sworn in life, until the bitter end, to guard the path that leads to death and becoming of the spirit. None would dare to venture close, for all of them feared it.

The servant to the undying flame, Crash the Collider is my name. My horn will sound and pierce like heat the icy heart of evil's keep. My scarab steed will fly on flames that trail behind and scorch the planes. Volcanoes erupting and explosions of light will make my path an impossible plight. No shadow will escape me, no spirit shall they smite. I was made by Nema, but renounced Her name and joined the company of Prion and his aggregates.

Meaning/Stage: time for change, a new adventure begins, be creative, enthusiastic, courageous, confident

Reversal: lacks motivation, careless, cowardly, retirement, step aside, it's someone else's turn

The Rhino and the Scarab: Fire signs, less evolved forms, all properties.

Personality traits: explorer, seeker, motivated, positive growth, inhibited, fickle, corruptible, naïve, impulsive, forgetful

THE BEARER OF FIRE
(KNIGHT OF WANDS)

The Bearer carried the arrow passed down from on high. The ancestors of all have drawn on its power. An entire race of fantastic creatures was born in dimensions just outside of our own.

> I am Acha. My arrow can travel through the fabric of time and kill every darkness that Nema designs. My companion, the eagle, with lightning bolts in his talons can rend mighty ravines in the shroud of the shadow. Together we travel on swift rays of sunlight. We will enter this world, then retreat into solace. I am a pure being made by Prion, but upon entering this temporal realm, I am infected with Time and am forced to run all of my long life, from Nema's evil clutches.

Meaning/Stage: positive headway, rewards for action and passionate engagement, charming, self-confident, daring, adventurous, passionate

Reversal: superficial, cocky, foolhardy, restless, hot-tempered, reluctant and timid

Sagittarius "The Archer"
(Born November 22nd*
-December 21st)
[* "pipe dreams," 7 of Cups]

Personality traits: laughter, loving, independent, caring, adaptable, trustworthy, restless, loud, desires understanding, application, healing, spiritual evolution, optimistic, happy, focused, exaggerates, concerned with status, mobile, hard-working, careless, disloyal, mediocre, delusional, clumsy, non-committal

Cusp sign: Aquila "The Eagle"
(Born December 17th
- December 25th)
Bearer of Crystal,
Mutable property.

THE KEEPER OF FIRE
(QUEEN OF WANDS)

The Lion is the king of the beasts and preserver of spirit; the sharp teeth and the razor-tipped claws give us ample reason to fear it.

I am Aseri, bold and resplendent, I radiate power. The crow, my emissary, will fly back and forth from my tower, bringing me the essence of Prion in shards, and I will burn them in braziers or keep them in jars. I prefer to retain my throne high above all. My beauty is so glorious any would fall before me. The power to harness, but left to maintain. Of the trinity guardians, I'm the one with the mane. Perfect and poised to rule all who would bow and the rest will be spared, but only for now. Nema did not make me, but She stole my pride, and so my essence is drawn into the sun to hide, where the power of Prion burns away my mortality and a symbol I shall become, the queen and king of all the beasts.

Meaning/Stage: an independent spirit, willpower, the essence of impulse and passion, creative, inspiring, forceful, charismatic, bold

Reversal: dull, uninspiring, weak, reserved, overly dependent upon others

Leo "The Lion"
(Born July 23rd-August 22nd)

Personality traits: confident, energetic, passionate, intense, generous, creative, controlling, arrogant, sometimes intolerant, desire to rule, emotional balance, finding purpose, egotism, letting go, responsible, strong, respectable, provider, severe, wrathful, clouded judgment, abrasive, unresponsive

Cusp sign: Corvus "The Crow"
(Born August 18th-August 26th)
Keeper of Crystal, Fixed property.

THE MASTER OF FIRE
(KING OF WANDS)

The ram, who with horns made of igneous stone, curved like a sword bent to cut through the bone, with eyes breathing fire and the power of spirit, no Cro-Magnon man would ever go near it. Until one day the greatest of hunters approached the destroyer and asked to be blessed.

After battle ensues and the warrior survives me, I, the ram, become tame and give the hunter new power, and say; "My representative among men you shall be, I will crown you with fire and none shall defeat you. And when your time is passed, I will see that you are blessed with an epic last battle and a warrior's death." Sitting between the furnaces of the planet, Ammram the destroyer is my name. I am the anger of spirit. To BE is to radiate the essence of life. I was created by Nema, but in a shallow breath, the star expanded and the seed of Prion fell and struck me between my eyes, and I knelt to the power of the one true God, digging a hole and planting the seed of another crystal tree.

Meaning/Stage: sexual energy, pure and true, attractive, wholehearted, energetic, cheerful, self-assured, genuine, powerful

Reversal: be honest with yourself, own yourself and become self-actualized

Aries "The Ram"
(Born March 21st-April 19th)

Personality traits: active, quickly aroused, pioneering spirit, impatient, selfish, egotistical, desire to lead and manage, adventurous, learns through experience, expansion, individuality, discernment, persistence, conceit, intolerance, choleric, enthusiastic, brilliant, fertile spirit, imaginative, ugly, empty, lethargic, depressive, doubting, weak-willed, self-loathing, pessimistic, tired, inconsistent, foolhardy, daredevil, extremist, bigot

Cusp sign: Orion "The Hunter"
(Born April 15th-23rd)
Master of Crystal,
Cardinal property.

CHAPTER 3
THE EPIC OF EARTH
"DO"

PIT

Through the smoke a silver cord did form. They followed it into the ground. Become they did, material of Prion's perfect sound.

In the opening between the eyes, sits the soul, and behind this power resides a depthless hole. The hole seems to drop into nothing forever, but there is a bottom just beyond the nether. Passing through membranes and entering wombs, each one giving birth to another dark room. Until finally, opening into the light, not the light of the spirit but the brilliance of sight, our spirits had followed the cord into material being, with new bodies to hold us and bright eyes for seeing.

Meaning/Stage: a feeling of loss, total emptiness, a lack of resources, falling away from reality

Reversal: entering into a new realm of riches and power, establishment of home and body

THE ALTAR TO THE ESSENCE OF EARTH
(ACE OF PENTACLES)

The altar to this essence was the physical of BEING, DOING and proceeding, parting ways and then re-meeting.

The joys and the pleasures of having been made flesh, we are trying once more to become one manifest. The sensation of touch and the feeling of Being leads us to Do because touching and seeing are just not enough; we are drawn to Do more. The entirety of our existence is born from the womb of the essence and the seed of the pure. Every atom of being is designed to endure. It is Nema who fills every atom with Time. Upon our creation all the essence was primed to decay and relent, but with Prion's intent, every atom is able to reproduce itself forever.

Meaning/Stage: completeness, contented, having all one desires, wealth, riches, resources, body, material, matter, all things tangible, material force, prosperity, practicality, new luck, health, being grounded, establishing a home, sprouting roots, creating something tangible, planting, cultivation, trust, a seed with which to plant one's dreams, the Philosopher's Stone

Reversal: empty, barren, loss of perspective, destitution, nothing to hold on to

CHANGING COURSES
(2 OF PENTACLES)

Hands were busy conjuring the planets and their moons, manipulating creation as their bodies came in bloom.

Juggling the universe, designing all its flaws, though making it imperfect, we build it to be strong. The creatures that will inhabit every corner of our Space, we design first as adults, and then their children will take their place. Reproducing just as quickly as Time could ever consume them, Prion will replace them as Nema's death removes them. The balancing act of maintaining existence requires patience, perseverance and ample resistance. Nothing can be unmade that once made is made, for though Time can consume them their spirits will remain.

Meaning/Stage: prepared to begin a great project, putting forth effort, collecting resources, an organized effort, flexibility, writing, balancing, instinctive knowledge of how to juggle multiple tasks, relief is on the way- you will not have to juggle forever, opportunity

Reversal: inability to perform, cannot bring together various aspects of life

COMPLETING ENDEAVORS
(3 OF PENTACLES)

Together they'd created something new, divined from the embodied spirit. It would always be a symbol. It would make the empty full. Immediately upon realizing She was alive, the Earth sat up and picked the loose dirt from betwixt her toes. She shook her mane and yawned and stretched. She worshipped at the feet of her mother and father.

> The Earth is now given a sense of itself, like a spirit is given a body in which to dwell. We will work in unison to build a paradise on this third planet from the sun…the final resting place of we, the children of the universe. This galaxy will become one of great importance and a sacred sanctuary for every form of life. Others will travel from distances greater than the space between stars to see the Eden we've created here.

Meaning/Stage: commitment to an idea loyal to a cause, the recipe is complete, teamwork, planning, competence, creating something that brings patrons on pilgrimage to see and worship it, being recognized for ones talents and receiving new work because of mastery, using treasured gem stones and working to sculpt an effigy with them, a commitment to excellence, accomplishment

Reversal: inability to work together to achieve something greater, resignation, surrender, abandonment of one's great work

SECURING POSSESSIONS
(4 OF PENTACLES)

They built upon foundations, looking towards the eastern sun. There'd be many new beginnings. They would cherish every one. After the roots were set and time had dug in its heels, Eon and Iode sat in silent repose. Iode held her prize, deep down inside, not long now before four new gifts would arrive.

Together, we've built a palace, a tribute to the altar upon which our future has been conceived. Now we will wait and enjoy the abundance of the nature we've designed. The shards of Prion are many to be found as they've been ground into earth that has never been touched. Perfect and shining, among the great mountains, the valleys are filled with green, mossy fountains.

Meaning/Stage: selfish use of resources for personal gain, clinging to your treasures, walls, structure, treasure trove, possessiveness, control, blocked, change, fear of loss, clinging to what you have acquired, unwilling to change, miserly, hoarding, building a foundation, burying treasure, solidity

Reversal: generous and detached from material wealth, a charitable disposition

EMPTY HANDS
(5 OF PENTACLES)

Then would come the hard times and suffering severe. By the time it all was over neither one could shed a tear.

The twisting of roots and the falling of snow create hardened soil, endless toil without growth. The shock of it sudden, the serpent entwines, and we, the children of Prion, are strangled with vines. The shadow has taken a hold of our bodies. It's clear to see Nema has no mercy to give. Matter is made of the temporal realm, most easily affected and infected by Her shadow. Our spirits She cannot touch if She tries, but the body and its feelings are how living dies. This is Her power, these Her advantages. Matter, although Prion's, is Nema's to take.

Meaning/Stage: losing resources or position, tangled roots and soil grasping at nothingness, decay, hard times, ill health, rejection, bad luck, a set-back, severe loss, things will get better, for now we must accept difficulty, poverty

Reversal: competition yields better results and you will find satisfaction, great expectations, although chances seem slim your needs and wishes will eventually be fulfilled

GENEROUS PROVISIONS
(6 OF PENTACLES)

So both were then forgiving, showering charity and love. They were blessed now, entitled by the powers from above.

All things pass when the power within overcomes all that isn't with what always has been. The strength of purgation through power and light sends the angry shadow roaming in the dead of the night. Storms will rise and tear the skies and shadows made of clouds will cry, but the Earth is created to draw from these storms the essence of moisture in life giving forms. The seeds will grow trees and the trees will bear fruit and the world will rejoice in abundance and all that grows new. We bestow upon nature its own cornucopia, endless fruition to share with its children.

Meaning/Stage: charitable, grateful for what one has, material gain, replenishment, to have or have not, excess of resources, unbound to material, ability to give away all one has to help others, knowledge, power, generosity, balance and perfection are maintained by stripping away what is not needed and allowing others to benefit from it, in a lesser sense—like scraps at a table thrown to the dog, gifts, scholarships

Reversal: running on empty, a lack of what is needed, begging, receiving monetary aid

DOUBTING FRUITION
(7 OF PENTACLES)

The seven seeds were planted and the tree of crystal grew. The waiting was the hardest part but truth would spring forth soon.

The seed of the tree which has already grown is in the other dimension, preceding the throne. Each element has its own world within which we, the children of Prion, will have to begin. Not until all of the elements have been collected can the realms come together and all be corrected. A septet of seeds, each makes a sound and the chain of vibrations will enter the ground. Germinate the seed of the crystal tree—planted by Prion, His final release. It is now revealed that the seed is His mind, which He placed here on earth for the seekers to find. It's the earthbound connection to the cloud of the souls. It's a vision of heaven for wise men and fools.

Meaning/Stage: impatient, waiting for a reward that may not come, cultivating a garden, effort towards hopes and goals, investment, assessment, reward, direction, change, you cannot control the situation—only watch and see what transpires now—you have done all that you can, waiting for fruit to ripen, learning patience, its out of your hands now- you must wait to see if your investment pays off, anxiety

Reversal: barren landscape, unyielding efforts, failure, misfortune, bad choices

DEEP INVOLVEMENTS
(8 OF PENTACLES)

Deep involvement in the patterns they established as they went, they turned mindset into progress as they made their world grow.

And so hope springs eternal and all are devoted to seeing their efforts bursting forth, then unloaded so they can spring forth again, and by doing so, become the power that undoes the shadow of Time. Focusing attention in sacred rituals and places, we're creating new temples in wide-open spaces. These places will be homes where the avatars come to replenish their powers and remember their names. Nema will be undone by the power of Prion, here in these humble spaces filled with inspiration and the potency of life. A place to worship the power of action, creation, elation and ultimate satisfaction.

Meaning/Stage: confidence, power and the ability to overcome, becoming one with your task, endeavoring to do something to the best of your ability, diligence, knowledge, details, apprenticeship, starting over, expanding upon the old roots, a time of learning and mistakes—but making these mistakes gracefully and with a willingness to learn from them, you've made the move—now stick with it, continue to cultivate it, persevere, follow through, have faith in yourself, prudence

Reversal: second-guessing, pessimism, doubts, languishing, depressed

GAINING GROUND
(9 OF PENTACLES)

Everything was cared for; all that lived were quite content. In splendorous surroundings they awaited their true intent.

Surrounded by gardens and splendorous flowers, ivory columns and great golden towers, a ziggurat is raised at the end of the path and the worm of Her shadow is unable to pass. Laying waste and eggs and forming our world, then Nema goes to sleep inside of herself. The entirety of creation is perfect and safe. We surround our opulent natures with grace. So now it is time to give birth to the signs; they are godlings, the sigils of elements prime. Each one will experience a life all alone, then together forever the Earth will they roam. The grandchildren of the almighty Prion, these blessings, once realized, will be without flaw. Mighty and mysterious, no one will ever know how each one reached adulthood and the adventures that they'll share.

Meaning/Stage: clinging to resources, fear of loss, prepared for the worst but hoping for and expecting the best, bringing something new into the world but fearing for its future, trying to protect something but realizing you cannot, discipline, self-reliance, refinement, watching over the blossoming world, retreat from the pace of life into a private world of pleasure, payment received, enough of everything you need and want, a pampered existence, sheltered, increase

Reversal: self-sacrifice, letting go, aborting a mission, allowing something to grow beyond your control, releasing your hold on something that never really belonged to you, accepting that you are no longer needed, moving on

REACHING PEAKS
(10 OF PENTACLES)

All that one could ask for was arranged to spare the Time. Now they represented the power of Prion, acting in his name.

Our kingdom is constructed of life and material, filled with the power of Prion the ethereal. Now we are full, our essences overflowing, the ten shards collected into a castle now growing. The planet, the power of all one can touch, of all that can be named and labeled as such, is now mastered and given a place and a name and from here all the happenings of our world became. But not into motion, nothing is set, there is more to unlock and more challenges to be met. So we sit here, enthroned enjoying our home, a ball of mud made to bring forth the life from our bones. The planet upon which all who'll live soon will roam.

Meaning/Stage: overwhelmed by opulence, having all one could ever need, preparing for the future of ones heirs, pleasant times, reciprocation, repayment, getting back all that you put in plus more, profit, affluence, permanence, convention, the pinnacle of prosperity, this can be passed on to your children, enough to last a lifetime, riches

Reversal: nothing is earned from all your hard work, strain and difficulty, over-spending, wastefulness, financial mistakes, bankruptcy

THE STRONGHOLD OF EARTH
(THE SUBTERRANEAN HALL)

An enclosure of Earth emerged. The powers that BE unlocked the door. Now the will to DO impelled them to go in search of something more.

> A wide fissure opens and a chasm becomes, that draws inward deepest breaths and from acts thoughts are made. This earthen enclosure will house and give life to all of the fae, every fairy, elf or dwarf that did neither god make. Every abstraction of living every monstrous beast, every phantom, every abnormal, godlike power is a mutation created within this green tower. Nema uses Prion to toy with the living, making all kinds of beings beyond Prion's willing. Humans are among the very last beings to be made from the essence of earth in the effigy of we, the demiurges: Eon and Iode. We were made not by Nema, but by Prion's will to be the one true purity among Her offenses. The white tiger and the gnome warrior will raise the Apothecary, our earthen child, here- in this sacred place.

Meaning/Stage: home of the body, a place where physical reality is of the utmost importance

Reversal: a place out of touch with reality, impractical and hopelessly empty

THE ACOLYTE OF EARTH
(PAGE OF PENTACLES)

The satyr, a minion of Nema at first, used riddles to coax and his flute to coerce.

I am often times martyred in the name of my lust, but if my heart is buried in the earth's magic crust, I will spring back, reborn and then find my horned steed. My stag will convey me to the realm of the trees. My music and scent and my countenance make me the perfect object of desire. Freed from a sleep by a fruit of the crystal tree, I the satyr, named Orphi, have become the Acolyte and guardian of the path through the forest of endless slumber. None come to the temple without my permission. None will know the pleasures of the deep wood without first hearing my song.

Meaning/Stage: an adolescent, full of desire, have an effect, be practical, prosperous, trusting and trustworthy, beginning of work, clever use of resources

Reversal: wastrel, pointless misuse of assets, flippancy, a lack of self-control

The Satyr and the Stag: Earth signs, less evolved form, all properties.

Personality traits: effecting, industrious, patient, self-aware, capable, responsible, clever, stubborn, pig-headed, materialistic, reckless, lustful, over-enthusiastic, pushy, unrefined, bad manners, slovenly

THE BEARER OF EARTH
(KNIGHT OF PENTACLES)

The virgin Imgyne, born of Prion, perfect and divine of wisdom and able to manipulate the world around her, was exiled to the most secret of woodlands where the long ferns grow, so that Nema could not taint her.

> I've fallen in love with my protector who is sworn not to touch me else I'll vanish forever. He is the shepherd who drives the great bears across the sky. He can speak with the beasts and can hear my heart. We travel as one, to and fro across the planet, bringing springtime to the world that has long slumbered. My crown of golden virtue gives me protection from Time's spell. I have the powers of the Fae and the magic to repel age and violence. All that see me forget my face. My eyes are filled with light, like a phantom of the night and wings of silvery glass adorn my back. I am always kept in a secret place, for to see me is to invite the judgment of fate. Those eyes impure that gaze upon me will soon be changed and speak nevermore.

Meaning/Stage: a pure and powerful presence, unwavering, cautious, thorough, realistic, hardworking, capacity for attainment, focus & fulfillment

Reversal: stubborn, unadventurous, obsessive, pessimistic, grinding, incapacity, failure, preoccupied, easily persuaded, lack of focus

Virgo "The Virgin"
(Born August 23rd-September 22nd)

Personality traits: practical, analytical, neat, industrious, detail-oriented, problem solver, conscientious, accusatory, judgmental, cynical, shy, worries too much, critical, perfectionist, unhealthy, slovenly, hoarder, vulnerable, exploitative

Cusp sign: Bootes "The Herdsman/ Bear Driver"
(Born September 18th -September 26th)
Bearer of Photons, Mutable property.

THE KEEPER OF EARTH
(QUEEN OF PENTACLES)

Tamed only by the rumblings of heaven itself, the protector of Earth is the bull called Vasti.

Using my horns and swollen udders to destroy the great walls of earth separating the seas from the land- I, Vasti, created the lakes and rivers that allow the world to drink and the earth mother's blood to circulate. The dogs of such ferocious power will watch over me as I make my throne in a patch of earth, dug in beside the wood and on the outskirts of the wide-open land. Great plains are mine to roam freely, and to release my hermaphroditic milk. I am the only bull ever to release such nourishment unto the planet, and it will cause the first spring, and then the seasons will begin turning in cycles. Even though I rarely move, sitting stalwart in my position, none would dare approach or tempt my fury.

Meaning/Stage: stoic, stalwart and immovable, motherly, nurturing, bighearted, down-to-earth, resourceful, trustworthy, compassionate, protective

Reversal: materialistic, pessimistic, stubborn, unforgiving, inhibited, condescending, depressive, self-centered, uncomfortable, indifferent, callous, fatalistic, suspicious

Taurus "The Bull"
(Born April 20th-May 20th)

Personality traits: warm, loving, gentle, charming, stable, dependable, practical, conventional, determined, patient, hard-working, methodical, opinionated, careful, enterprising, adept, supportive, steady, jealous, possessive, lazy, slow, clumsy, inconsistent, indecisive, neglectful, hesitant

Cusp sign: Canus Major (& Canus Minor) "The Great Dog"
(Born May 16th-May 24th)
Keeper of Photons, Fixed property.

THE MASTER OF EARTH
(KING OF PENTACLES)

Regivian the primeval—she is the grandest of mutations and the essence of the Earth, child to the mother of nature accompanied by her shrewd and clever companion.

Her horns are overflowing with the abundance of the planet and her hooves bleed flowers awash in crystalline dew. Her scales and tail enable her to navigate the planet's veins, and trees and moss and plants and flowers all give thanks to her for power. She radiates the scent of growth; her gaze surpasses the densest wood. She watches over all that grows and gives unto us life and song. Her fox, her friend, will bring her jewels all drawn from caves and limpid pools. The vines and leaves that cascade down surround her horns and make her crown. She is the earthen child of spring, the seed of life in everything. Mother nature's perfect spawn, master of the power whence she was drawn.

Meaning/Stage: great physical presence, mystical, secret powers, watery breath, enterprising, adept, reliable, supporting, steady, what is obvious, plain as the nose on your face, no surprises

Reversal: lazy, clumsy, inept, unreliable, neglectful, inconsistent, hidden motives, conspiracy, suspect

Capricorn "the Sea Goat"
(Born December 22nd -January 19th)

Personality traits: nurturing, big-hearted, down-to-earth, resourceful, trustworthy, conservative, strong work ethic, dedicated, dutiful, serious, responsible, practical, sense of purpose, steadfast, planner, ambitious, materialistic, pessimistic, stubborn, unforgiving, inhibited, condescending, depressive, self-centered, uncomfortable, indifferent, callous, fatalistic, suspicious

Cusp sign: Vulpecula "The Fox"
(Born January 15th –23rd)
Master of Photons, Cardinal property.

CHAPTER 4
THE ANECDOTE OF AIR
"THINK"

SILENCE

Enter thought; the only voice the MIND couldn't stop. The clouds were full of storms and stars. The journey there was never far.

The silver cord, it snaps in twain and the nostrils of space inhale the remnant energies. Formed from the spirit's interaction with the material world, the mind and soul create themselves at the behest of our will. A deep well into the stars, so deep that none can reach its zenith. The endlessness of thought is revealed. It stretches even beyond the veil into the spaces in between, where nothing knows what something means. In the tunneling void the sorrow pierces to the core, the very moment that our souls were born. From that point on the sorrow swells and the soul grows restless and tired of its constricting mortal coil.

Meaning/Stage: a sense that you are being whisked away beyond your control, sudden, usurping, an interruption, all of your memories and thoughts are nullified by a sudden burst of divine power, relocation of spirit, body and mind are imminent

Reversal: a vortex or passageway leading to a powerful revelation

THE ALTAR TO THE ESSENCE OF AIR
(ACE OF SWORDS)

The truth that pierced every veil was the power of reason to prevail. A sharper brain would still retain what the memory and the meaning changed. The power of reason was to behold what's infinitely possible.

> The never-ending chain of thoughts and dreams are what perception's wrought upon our minds. It takes its toll and corrugates our precious souls. It pokes our bodies full of holes and draws forth the sorrows when we are full. The first tears shed portend the fate of elements not yet incarnate. Remembrances of things forgotten and the many sorrows of ages past; think upon them, dwell deeply and consider what contemplation can reveal. Words of wisdom, sounds of pain, the utterances are unrestrained. From out our eyes vibrate our souls. Come listen now, come hear them spin and sing the wind to sleep. Slumber mind, and now we dream. Our shadows come from in between to torment us and take our peace. With knowledge comes power, but also grief.

Meaning/Stage: seeking truth, cynical but ready to receive and believe, mistrust and an innate need to find out for oneself, the power to find "truth" in any given situation, mental force, truth, justice, awakening of the mind, sharp and clear perception, ideas, dreams, a test, fortitude, great expectations for the future, desires and ideas yet to manifest, impetus, Excalibur—the sword of truth

Reversal: fixated and without motivation or inspiration, falsehood, a veil of lies and misdirection, obsession with one way of thinking

PEACE OF MIND
(2 OF SWORDS)

Peace was meditation, prone to focus on that which was not known. When gone unchecked it still had grown. The time would come to bleed the stone.

Her essence still remains above it, lingering there and hovering. But, out of sight and out of mind, forgetfulness can be divine. So we cross our swords, we breathe in deep and exhale the breath that precludes sleep. Consider all we've learned thus far and focus on the farthest star. This meditation brings a truce, a way to never have to choose between two evils. Neither suits, so we hold our tongues, and pretend we're mute. Let float the petals on the wind and pay no mind to where they've been. We stay adrift on our own clouds and open our eyes when the wind stops blowing.

Meaning/Stage: distraught and torn between two directions, but stopping to assess and regroup. The calm before the storm arrives, a time of peace balanced by the threat of what is yet to come, a waiting period, on the brink of unpredictability, blocked emotions, avoidance, stalemate, the knowledge of compromise, differing ideas, keeping the peace, confused and cyclical thinking that must be constrained, balance

Reversal: decisive action without deliberation, a mistaken sense of clarity, jumping to conclusions, discord

RELEASE OF SORROWS
(3 OF SWORDS)

A perfect sorrow, meant to be, like pleasure, pain was God in three. The Shadow played a wicked game. She mimicked love, and love was to blame.

It's time to make decisions now about where to make incisions, how deep, and where they'll mar the least and give the pain a quick release. There will be scars, some unseen, some break the world apart it seems. Some tear the heartstrings at their seams, and leave a mark, a wound unclean. Beware the pain that comes with truth supposed by a mind uncouth. There is no universal accord. The truths we make are only ours. Beware perception, misconception and the plague of misdirection meant to lead us down the path of storms and ruin... THUNDERCLAP!

Meaning/Stage: sorrow, pain and mental anguish, something comes between us, it is our perception and thus we can never have a complete accord, heartbreak, loneliness, betrayal, peace doesn't last and the inevitable has arrived, wrong ideas, hurtful words, lies exposed, the guise falls, disappointments, separation, schism, bad timing, loss

Reversal: creation of space, splitting things so they may expand beyond their boundaries, left alone to widen your scope of vision, a divergence of the minds, disagreement

GENTLE SLUMBERS
(4 OF SWORDS)

They rested within their comfort cloud that drowned away the thinking sounds. It transformed turmoil into peace and drifted upwards towards release.

We enjoy this time bereft of stress and use this moment to digress. Reflecting upon what's come to pass, we draw on power from our nest. What's coming next is of no concern, what matters now are bridges burned and roads not taken left behind. They're laid at ease upon our minds. Weary, numb and taciturn, the mouth won't move but the words still churn inside our heads, until we're dead. The voice will never leave unsaid what must be thought, nor what may be secret even unto we who see it. Leave it all behind for now, just float and soak, unfurl our brows. Everything just seems to stop. The world shrinks and seems to drop away into the starry black. From where we are going we won't come back.

Meaning/Stage: peaceful, at rest, meditative, sensory deprivation allows the mind to clear itself of rampant thoughts and unwanted stimuli, rest, contemplation, quiet, preparation, meditation, recuperation, rebuilding inner power, preparation for future battle, fixed time to heal, blinding oneself, denying truth, hiding from something, ignoring the obvious, healing

Reversal: truth, facing consequences, admitting something to yourself, a rude awakening, no rest for the weary, reality check

OPPOSING FORCES
(5 OF SWORDS)

Evil came in many forms, familiar and frightening, flying in swarms. The Queen of Shadows sent her spawn to break then kill and eat the dawn.

We feel the darkness coil and squeeze so tightly that we cannot breathe. Her many arms and many heads will leave all in her pathway dead. The sounds, Her words, they still resound all blended with the fangs and frowns. Her swords cut deep, like words; they swirl around and round as they cut us to ribbons. There is no defense against the blades. They slice our wings and feathers fray. We fall and plummet, from the sky, so vast. Cruelty fills it, glimmering with the blood it's spilled. Fear is but remembered pain, and the unknown power of reason's bane.

Meaning/Stage: swarming troubles, defeat is on the horizon but nevertheless—you must persevere, others are counting on you, an indefatigable foe, unnatural forces coming together to engineer your downfall, self-interest, discord, dishonor, after a battle—being forced to retreat because you are overpowered by a more willful person, good does not always win, they had an unfair advantage, a pointless struggle you have to learn from and cut your losses, over-reaching, defeating oneself by exerting too much force

Reversal: defeating enemies, overcoming negative thoughts, victory in the face of overwhelming defeat, a good last-minute decision

BALANCED CROSSINGS
(6 OF SWORDS)

A smooth retreat with experienced sails, the clouds remitted them through the gales. They went in search of new horizons, safe from all the dark inside them.

> Though it gives chase, we have put distance in between us, calm and listless. Storms are brewing just behind us, but we are lost, they'll never find us. It's time to travel, to find a shore where no one seeks to make a war. There's much to be found across the expanse, over the next horizon. We'll heal and lick our wounds away and view the world with the dawning day. Propelled towards fate and new resolve all fear is destined to dissolve. We'll find the winds of change we seek across the sky as the clouds' curls peak. We row our tiny ship to shore, and seek out what fate has in store.

Meaning/Stage: deflated, exhausted, meandering towards the horizon in search of sanctuary, one must find a place to hide and recollect, they will be looking for you so it's best to move swiftly, hidden sadness, recovery, travel, leaving difficulties behind, a solution to the puzzle or problem, riddles, the answer to the enigma lies on the distant shore, walking away, a time to travel and forget, out of sight- out of mind, solutions

Reversal: difficult journey, evading, on the run, escape, running the gauntlet in retreat

FALSE NOTIONS
(7 OF SWORDS)

Soon enough they'd come to claim,
and battle they would to maintain
a healthy wealth of thoughts to use,
an armory of bladed truth.

We fight and struggle with what we know. Our knowledge serves us well for now. But someone's always smarter yet, you may not know it but regret is how they distract you long enough to make you think that you're too tough. Then, like a snake with bladed wings, they slip between the cracks and sting with venomous fangs. But the poison fails, and they grab those serpents by their turbid tales and cut their heads off clean and fast, and leave behind their shadowed pasts. Prevail upon the enemy to never try and stab at thee. The power yields to swords, not shields, so cut them down and make them kneel. We have the power to win the day, though violence now must be the way.

Meaning/Stage: a feeling of strength despite your intuition that this is a battle that is unwinable, enraged, you lash out at all who would dare confront you, facing the giant without fear, running away, suspicion, hidden dishonor, a thief is stealing from you, trying to defeat you while you are vulnerable- attacking your ideas, they are spreading gossip about you and you are unable to be there to defend yourself, to catch a thief you must be a thief, to win in this battle you will have to take a circuitous route, broken truce, intruders invade the sacred ground, sneak attack, distraction

Reversal: integrity, honor, facing unparalleled odds with dignity and courage, you believe you can win this battle- all it requires is time and dedication to the cause. No surprises here

TIGHT SURROUNDINGS
(8 OF SWORDS)

They were overcome by a cage of sabers that cut them deeply and made them bleed. They could not break the spell of anguish, could not think and could not see.

It's come to this, a final stand against the legion of shadow's hands. Endless blackness whence they came, they're ceaseless in battle, failing shame. Nothing left to give at all; this is how we, the twin demiurges, fall. Overwhelmed by Nema's wrath, we cannot defeat or match the numbers and the thoughts of pain that Her paragons lay us to blame. Giving up is the only choice. To fight is but to lose our voice. But what voice matters in a cage, no bird will sing, and God will age. The evil cadre comes to claim us, rip and tear, to scar and maim us. This is a victory for the black. She gave us life now She takes it back. The hopelessness that comes with thought will make the most divine distraught. The shadow bearer of ill news, there's nothing we can say or do.

Meaning/Stage: disappointment, fear, anguish and anxiety over the future, bad news, omens, restriction, confusion, powerlessness, damned if you do, damned if you don't- take the risk, do what you have to in order to escape this situation, you can't be afraid to move even if it means you will be cut or lose something in the process- that is inevitable now, the blindfold and ropes that bind are fear, you must dispel fear in order to escape, you must endure the torture, the cuts, the loss- in order to be freed, trusting fate, following the path to its intended end without fear or regret, blind faith, imprisonment

Reversal: coming to grips with doubt, disbelief, feeling forsaken, being blinded and left in the dark, consumed by fear and anxiety. No structure or foundation upon which to feel comfortably stable, freedom

SOUL SPLINTERS
(9 OF SWORDS)

Tortured, broken, minds in ruin, lost inside a maze of nightmares. They could not escape from madness. Everything was fear and sadness.

Beaten, battered left to rot and soak up all the frightening thoughts. What will become of both our souls? We're kept alive while they're drilling holes into our brains and causing everlasting pain. The riddle of a mortal life is that death is why we were designed. To live and think and learn to feel, the tear is a scar becoming real. Feelings are starting to invade now that memories pervade. Attachment claims the mind for naught and rips it apart to find what's sought. The shadow finds that anguish fuels the essence of Time, calm and cruel. There's no escape from your own brain She lives inside making us all insane!

Meaning/Stage: mental disorder, paranoia, dark thoughts, depression, there is no way out, you are trapped, worry, guilt, anguish, multitude of troubles, nightmares, blowing things out of proportion, overwhelmed by guilt and mental issues, its all in your head, its all just a bad dream, you must realize this in order to cope with it all effectively, helplessness, despair, spiraling downward, battle

Reversal: peaceful acceptance, a necessary evil overcome, daydreams and visions of peace and pleasure, do not deceive yourself, embrace the pain

SHATTERED HOPES
(10 OF SWORDS)

Given up, all hope was lost. The sun was rising, melting frost. The dawn revealed their final fate, their consciousness beyond the gate.

At the shores of death we do repent and find out why we were so sent by fate to meet our certain doom. For Nema cannot be removed, denied, avoided or escaped. This is the way the cosmos were shaped. The egg of God is cracked and bursts and shards of Prion burn the curse away. And now our bodies change, renewing our forms and giving us names. One is female. One is male. All creatures henceforth will avail from all the suffering we've endured, androgynous or other forms. Our minds are separate though once one. Our lives of feeling have begun. All along we have been made, two halves together, night and day. We form a union now complete. The final element is released. It's always darkest before the dawn. Let come what may, for we'll be gone.

Meaning/Stage: the worst is over, welcoming the decisive end to an agonizing battle, a death of sorts—but not of the body, of the mind, finality, a succession of natural occurrences that leads ultimately to illumination, bottoming out, victim, mentality, martyrdom, everything goes wrong, the world comes crashing down—but in the end, although all is ruined, it has given you a new start, free of all fear and worry because you can't be "more dead" than you are now, it is time to be reborn anew, weightless and without concern, the sun is rising in the distance, struggle ends, floundering, being swallowed by the blackness forever, ruin

Reversal: celebration, passing through difficulty, rebirth, a conclusion to worries, allowing things to settle and all returns to "normal" (whatever that is), an end to distress

THE CITADEL OF CLOUDS
(THE CASTLE IN THE SKY
THE ABODE OF AIR)

As sharp and swift as lightning crawled, the crystal abode was formed from storms. The key unlocked the passageway that led to where the heart was born.

> The atmosphere all filled with energies unseen. Dimensions between dimensions and invisible creatures not known to us reside within the currents of air. The Scientist will be born among the clouds and reared by the sylph and the shimmering, blue dragon. Here the thoughts of all become heard, and those who can hear all of their voices must learn to filter through the tumult and focus on singularity. We are unlocking the realm of the mind, where the spirit germinates the soul and the soul creates memories. Our metamorphic wings appear and disappear at our whims. A sword to pierce and a compass to point will guide our way through the endless vastness of outer space. In the distance, the river of the souls of all who have ever lived shines like the purest diamond.

Meaning/Stage: a box of secrets within which you might stow away your deepest and most personal thoughts, a sacred space in the depths of your unconscious mind, where memories are kept and ideas are formed

Reversal: all you know and believe is revealed to the world, nothing is a secret anymore

THE ACOLYTE OF AIR
(PAGE OF SWORDS)

Ubularch the owl man and his gryphon took to the skies to protect the coalescing orb that came to our dimension from the nether realm.

My task is to keep watch over that which is constructed of the energies that would give birth to two nations of beings; the terrestrial Rodinians and the sunborn Andromedans. I am Ublarch, with the power to call down streaks of lightning and peals of thunder, and who carried the scimitar of gales. I have a tempestuous demeanor that is not to be trifled with. My crown will scrape the sky and the secret path towards the air temple will be held fast between my shinning talons. I'll cut you to ribbons if you try to trick me. If you cross into my territory your chances of survival are slim.

Meaning/Stage: old patterns, be inquisitive, use your mind, be truthful, be fair, have fortitude, obeys the rules, follows protocol, learning the ropes and enforces the law

Reversal: disobedient, rule breaker, iconoclast, loose cannon

The Owl and the Gryphon: Air signs, less evolved form, all properties.

Personality traits: logical, friendly, sociable, thoughtful, balanced, equitable, forthright, intelligent, superficial, opinionated, stubborn, moody, cold, judgmental

THE BEARER OF AIR
(KNIGHT OF SWORDS)

Brascelies was the sharp-feathered, two-headed, hooded serpent warlord, with tongues that darted through the air like spears. He carried the staff of knowledge and an antidote to Nema's poison.

I will rule over ancient civilizations and sacrifices will be made to appease my hunger. My guile beguiles even the smartest of foes, and I know just how to draw upon the power of the shadow void and use it to my advantage. Drawn into battle by the shadows attack, I defend those who worship me and destroy the powers that come to devour. My greatest prize, the unicorn; a perfect beast of purity, I keep at arms length with my tail coiled about it. The desert skies and the pyramids of blood will never fall, and the wind will whisper and whistle of the flying cobra's great power.

Meaning/Stage: duplicity incarnate, direct, authoritative, incisive, knowledgeable, logical, giving chase, pursuit of an ideal and willingness to fight for that which you believe to be true

Reversal: blunt, overbearing, cutting, opinionated, unfeeling, unsuccessful conflict, a time for expeditious retreat, let this one go

Gemini "The Twins"
(Born May 21st-June 20th)

Personality traits: optimistic, adaptive, willing to learn, inquisitive, versatile, impatient, restless, easily distracted, nervous, unstable, hyper critical

Cusp sign: Monoceros "The Unicorn"
(Born June 16th-24th)
Bearer of Plasma,
Mutable property.

THE KEEPER OF AIR
(QUEEN OF SWORDS)

Magnate, the luminary of souls, was a peacock of unbridled ostentation. Plumage that rivaled the purest of jasper and lapis lazuli, no jewel could compare. With a rapier wit and an ewer for pouring the contents of clouds into basins and fountains, the keeper of wisdom and unearthly knowledge could speak every language and create movement in mountains.

My kingdom is that of the fairies and falcons, the birds of the air and the songs of the free. A Pegasus, "Windhorse" the shamans will call him, is here at my side to avert strokes of anger. A balanced temperament to match my insightfulness, nothing can shake me. My stare can sunder stone. The wind whistles through towers of glass and obsidian and I recline and let the thunderheads shade me. I am a shining example of what power can be when wielded so effortlessly.

Meaning/Stage: thin, neglected body, intellectual, analytical, articulate, just, ethical, wise council, thought provoking, careful assessment and weighing of options

Reversal: without consideration, careless, wanton, slipshod, tuning others out

Aquarius "the Water Bearer"
(Born January 20th-February 18th)

Personality traits: honest, astute, forthright, witty, experienced, friendly, intuitive, original, inspiring, introspective, balanced, keen aesthetic, logical, magnanimous, temperamental, awkward, eccentric, unpredictable, picky, aloof, resentful, unreachable, cold, rude, fixated

Cusp sign: Pegasus
"The Winged Horse"
(Born February 14th-23rd)
Keeper of Plasma, Fixed Property.

THE MASTER OF AIR
(KING OF SWORDS)

The colossal king of dragons, Faze the wyvern, also called 'The Resister,' blew hot and dry wind easterly and even the desert blistered. Carrying heads of those dethroned by perfect justice dealt in swords, the fangs and claws did rend asunder sparing none his caustic words.

> I condemn the world of men, but then come soaring to its rescue. In the face of Nema's horde, their attacks I cannot eschew. With the aid of other dragons and the serpents of the stars, their weapons forged for justice are brought to tear the paragons apart. My crown of blades surrounding horns, I scream! I cry! The air is shorn, and comets fall. I cast a spell that locks their minds in brightest hell. I have stars for eyes, scales like iron, and an electric tail with a point refined for piercing through the void of Time and entering other dimensions. I am the scourge of other galaxies, when not engaged with the shadow beasts. Feathered wings as sharp as knives, I'll take away ten thousand lives.

Meaning/Stage: flamboyance and trendsetting, honest, astute, forthright, witty, experienced, cold indifference to pleas for mercy, fair and truthful advice

Reversal: ignorant, accusatory, refusal to listen, stubborn, unyielding, ruthless

Libra "the Scales/ Balances"
(Born September 23rd-October 22nd)

Personality traits: intellectual, analytical, articulate, just, ethical, social, cooperative, tactful, gracious, diplomatic, charming, refined

Reversal: sulking, superficial, loud, impulsive, impatient, dismissive

Cusp sign: Draco "The Dragon"
(Born October 18th-October 26th)
Master of Plasma,
Cardinal Property.

CHAPTER 5
THE WORDS OF WATER
"FEEL"

DROUGHT

The broken sky, a thunder strike, then, swirling as whirlpools—the bridge into Time their spirits took to be reborn as love incarnate. But before they could proceed they were overwhelmed by waves of joy and sadness, peace and gladness tears and laughter, never happy ever after.

Drying up like dying flowers, rivers of tears give our spirits their power to dwell and subsist among Time, which resists the essence of immortal Prion. Everything we've felt has been taken away. We have to relive it all day after day. Remembering every emotion we've had without knowing we've had them can drive us both mad. We are doomed to relive all the pleasure and pain and without any wisdom to give it a name. It aches and then dissipates, pulling us down through the drain of the universe wearing deep frowns.

Meaning/Stage: a feeling that one has no more tears left to cry, emotionally numb, nothing left, having been so emotive for so long, you can no longer feel much of anything and have become empty and listless, emotion bursts forth

Reversal: an outpouring of emotion, an utter deluge of feelings beyond your control

THE ALTAR TO THE ESSENCE OF WATER
(ACE OF CUPS)

Memories of love and perfect, unified creation were made for the joyous and the purposeful to live in bliss, rebellious. Every potent passion, every single throbbing tear filled their cups to overflowing spilling over love and fear. The feelings generated by the flowing of the waters affected them all in different ways; mothers, fathers, sons and daughters, lovers—perfect pairs of people committed to becoming equal, unified by emotion.

> The bottomless well that will never run dry. It's the hole in the heart of the spirit of life. The water cascades, pouring over and over. A creation of love, an abundance of feeling, embracing existence and the current of healing. The rhythm the heart beats in weeps for the spirit, as desire goes dancing and plays inspiration. Musing and using the drive and the zeal to be joined with sensation, made able to feel.

Meaning/Stage: creativity, love, compassion, pure imagination, free-flowing existence, undulation, reflection, ideas come with relative ease because they spring from your heart and require no analysis, enveloped in gratitude, an upwelling of feelings that creates deeper meanings for and attachments to: things, ideas and people, the Holy Grail

Reversal: loneliness and heartbreak, emptiness, apathy, to languish, stagnant puddles of unrealized expression, emotionally draining, stale

BLOSSOMING UNIONS
(2 OF CUPS)

Perfect and complete they were, and feeling every moment of it. They would become the spirits of the love that ruled the world.

The void hath overflowed and the dream cannot contain it all. It rains down pure emotion saturating both our hearts. The most amazing things we find in each other's eyes; mirror images reflecting what the other most desires. The fountain of youthful infatuation springs forth with gleeful spouts of joy. The crests of waves now carry us as we embrace beneath the stars. Union of blood, merging of spirit, sharing each other's deepest wishes. We swim in circles with the fishes and warm our lips with sweet, sweet kisses.

Meaning/Stage: romantic love, a perfect trust, cooperation, sharing dreams, working together, partnership, reliance, reciprocity, connection, truce, attraction, recognition of love, the two people's eyes meet, a soul mate, a swell of emotion, putting aside your selfish desires, union, love

Reversal: stepping away to gain perspective, singularity, loneliness, individuality, introspection, doing what you feel is best for you, looking out for "numero uno"

JOINING HANDS
(3 OF CUPS)

They celebrated everything in jubilant yet calm repose. It was a time for building memories and laughing of times now ever after.

Gathering the prism underneath the curling waves, we eat and drink and make quite merry, for tomorrow pours our watery graves. Ebullient and laughing loudly, joining together, toasting proudly the lives that we are living and all the years we've left to give. The party starts and all do dance. The sloshing water, like a hypnotic trance, induces three euphoric smiles. We talk and joke for just a while. We throw our heads back. Our arms are open wider than the endless ocean. Nothing can compare to fun when the working's over and the day is done.

Meaning/Stage: a party atmosphere, gathering, harmony, contented sigh, satisfaction, friendship, sisterhood, a reunion with friends and family, enjoy yourself, exuberance, community, happiness, togetherness, two cups pour into a third which overflows with love for all life, celebration, protection

Reversal: jealousy, envy, bitterness, competition, self-defeating mindset, suspicion, don't ruin everyone else's good time

EMBITTERED SWEETNESS
(4 OF CUPS)

Yet soon their purgatory yawned and needed to be reborn a seed, for the nectar of the everlasting had become the common drink.

We take for granted that which flows so readily and copiously. We lather in the grotto's bubbles, mulling over all our troubles. And though they are few, still they skew our view, for we are spoiled by easy living. Everyone is always giving. Self-indulgence takes its toll. We've had enough. Our bellies are full. So now forlorn and seeking satisfaction, we're waiting for a new reaction. Bored and dull the tedium swirls, like waiting for oysters to cough up pearls. We daydream now of what might have been and what is waiting just around the bend. They've all gone home, we're left alone to sit and wonder in the foam.

Meaning/Stage: ennui, dissatisfaction, lethargy, distraction, taking things for granted, overworking a project, you need to know when to stop, everything in moderation, self-absorption, apathy, going within, stagnation, boredom, restlessness, depression, over-indulgence, don't try to escape it—change it, musing, excess

Reversal: time to go searching, follow the signs, discomfort leads one to strike out on one's own and search for the elusive, time to get out of your rut

DEEP SIGHS
(5 OF CUPS)

Stumbling in a stupor, some regrettable steps were taken. Piercing pain, but not of body, it was their hearts that needed to be shielded.

Drunk on all that we can hold, a barrel empty, we lost control. The world starts spinning like a maelstrom and the sky starts pummeling us with hailstones. Ships are run aground and splintered by icy rain and fractured winter, melting only to freeze and then there's a salty, sea-born breeze again. Spilling out what's left of the wine, we've lost our taste for the power divine. The feelings that come after pure elation are disappointment and desolation. A taste of God is not enough. We cannot live without His touch in every single waking drop. When it melts away the feeling stops. We reel in pain born from above, the absence of His perfect love.

Meaning/Stage: loss, bereavement, regret, inner turmoil, guilty conscience, failure, self-loathing, a feeling of inadequacy, depression, giving up, loss, obsessing over what has been lost rather than being glad for what one still has, disappointment, falling short of expectations, how do I get past this? look at the good and stop focusing on the bad

Reversal: accept the things you cannot change and move forward, don't be so hard on yourself, set realistic goals, be willing to forgive yourself, focus on the positive and you will succeed, one step at a time

NOSTALGIC REFLECTIONS
(6 OF CUPS)

Containers of their joyful tears and memories that drowned the soul in blood within the music box that beat of perfect, nascent love.

Purity is our spring of living memories. From infancy to adolescence, our loving presences soak in the sunlight. Pooling ripples, cool and calm a pond of dreams of days long gone. The peace surpasses understanding arms to cradle, gentle landings. Birth of joy and splashing puddles, some are brazen some are subtle. Shy and hopeful smiles and laughter believe in happily ever after. Remembering together, holding hands, sitting in the soft, warm sand, we let the water lap our toes and watch the deluge overflow. It seeps between bricks and bursts through walls creating tiny waterfalls. The brooks and streams that fill our dreams reflect our souls, or so it seems.

Meaning/Stage: good will, innocence, childhood, passion, it is time to grow up and put away childish notions, pursuing infatuation does not lead to emotional fulfillment, innocence, nostalgic memories, puppy love, one's first and purest inclinations of love, reminiscing, getting lost in the past, naivety, trying to rekindle an idyllic feeling, foolish delusions

Reversal: emotional maturity is inherent, reflection on childhood is reassuring, recognizing past immaturity and how much you have grown since, being grateful for past emotional experiences without trying to recapture them

PIPE DREAMS
(7 OF CUPS)

Intoxicated by the fountain, every dream and fantasy became as real as their stormy imaginations could manifest.

Other spirits try to take possession of our souls in lacrimae. Libations of imagination let their senescence bleed into our spirits. Such wondrous dreams of what could be and all that one could ever want, they echo through our liquid brains and wallow in the minds they haunt. We cannot run, we cannot hide, from that which comes from deep inside. It follows us and soaks in deep. When we're awake they'll spring a leak and flood our world with phantom love. They know our hearts. They fit like gloves. They can manipulate our souls, so we mustn't be this fortune's fool. We must save ourselves from whims of fancy, setting our hearts on things less chancy.

Meaning/Stage: wishful thinking, options, dissipation, a time to entertain fanciful ideas and dreams, drop your inhibitions and be honest with yourself about your heart's desire, imaginings, unable to make up one's mind, fantasies, illusions, deceptions, none of these fantasies are real or as good as they seem, don't make a hasty decision, emote and hide nothing, truth

Reversal: recollect yourself, do not be fooled by daydreams or delusions of grandeur, illusion

Ophiuchus (Serpentarius) "the Serpent Bearer"
(Born November 29th-December 17th)

WITH RECKLESS ABANDON
(8 OF CUPS)

In an epic moment, facing monsters and disasters, they finally took the necessary steps to purify their soul's containers.

Massive swells raise walls of water, drowning worlds in epic slaughter. We wipe the slate and start again. Let's not look back at where we've been. The storm inside, where we are hiding, shows no signs that it's subsiding. No one's listening to our troubles. It's time to push forth, on the double. Across the shoreline the languid crawl, past tidal pools and violent squalls. We must avoid the crashing waves that pound and drown and dig men's graves. It's time to brave the deep unknown, to stick our oars into the foam and row until we can row no more, then dive in and swim for the farthest shore. Fear not for soon it will recede. Until then; stay afloat and remember to breathe.

Meaning/Stage: deeper meaning, moving on, restriction, pay attention to your own emotions and see to it that you are taking care of yourself else you cannot give love to others, weariness, shedding of old relationships, a new dream calls, leaving behind familiarity and comfort for a new adventure, a love who you now see on a deeper level than before, divorce from one emotional connection in favor of a new one, gaining the capacity for helping others by learning from your mistakes

Reversal: a time to walk away and create space, attending to your own emotional needs and refraining from trying to help others, a release from obligatory situations

SHADOWS OF LUCK
(9 OF CUPS)

The shards of ancient Prion overflowed their endless spirits and the powerful love remade them, and then they remade the world.

After following the stars and navigating constellations, we have come to find a castle beyond our wildest imaginations. Bejeweled with hearts and glistening cups all wet and dripping, falling upwards towards the heavens making clouds reflected in the arctic shroud. The ice is warm. A geyser forms and erupts with love like a bottle of champagne uncorked. We drink to happiness and pleasure, perfect peace, and a life of leisure. All the oceans pay respect to us, the demiurges. They collect and move the glacier to the edge between dimensions, known and yet unseen. The sounds of heaven aren't so distant. Here we bask in some of its brilliance.

Meaning/Stage: dream come true, sensuality, pleasure, release, an expression of happiness and contentment, satisfaction and emotional fulfillment, peace, happiness, satiation, love, gratitude, wishes granted, all you desire comes to you opportunely, entering heaven where the party has already begun—the wine glasses are filled and all your loved ones are waiting for you, the beginning of a happy ending, release

Reversal: the painful truth, nothing is going your way, wasted time and effort, bad luck, time to reconsider your situation, continuing with this will only lead to sadness

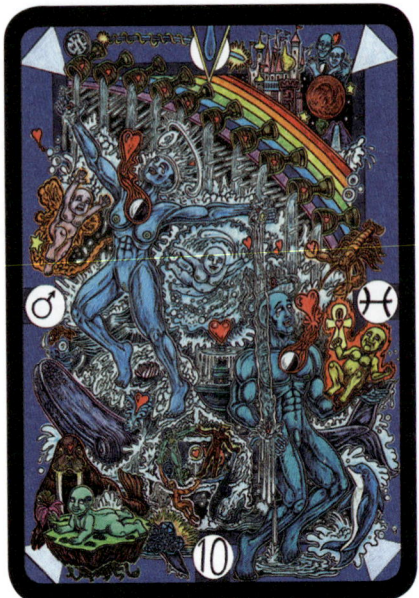

HALOS OF WARMTH
(10 OF CUPS)

Lifted into ecstasy, the ancient power of everything bestowed His greatest gifts upon them and all was everlasting.

Breach and breathe then dive straight down into this paradise we've found. We wrap ourselves in perfect peace, of hearts and dreams and love so deep. Profound and clear and unrestrained, the unconditional bliss remains forever and always to be a piece of mortal affection and emotion. There are so many feelings that we've shared. Some caused damage that's now repaired. All the tears we've ever wept along with stars that we have kept to dwell upon and always know, remembering that which does not show. The gratitude and joyous rapture, pouring out chapter after chapter, is leading to happily ever after, once upon a time. Family and friends soon gather. Arms are raised and none would rather live a life that's free of feeling, for though the pain is great the love is healing. Now here in heaven, forevermore, felicitation will endure.

Meaning/Stage: joy, peace, family, abundance, pure pleasure, a heavenly paradise, a perfect situation for all involved, a happy ending, trust, reliability, endless holiday, they come running out to greet you, smiles and love abound, cornucopia of peace and prosperity, absolute love and bliss, sublime ecstasy

Reversal: heartache, sorrow, emptiness, everything is spoiled, what could have been, a tormented existence, relapse, rejection, hopelessness

THE WHEREABOUTS OF WATER
(THE ETERNAL FOUNTAIN)

The path ended here, to reclaim the spirit, and through that door was the realm of Prion. Time was then an instant, and the happenings of eternity became all of your memories and mine.

The Tortoise and the Undine will raise the Philosopher within this tidal pool. Mastery of emotion is the only key to unlocking the watery gates, for the experience of mortality is pain and suffering coupled with joy and pleasure. An understanding of this balance and the ability to allow both aspects of this complexity to flow freely through you is the key to enduring the test of life. Without this, existence is empty. For the very purpose of Being is to Feel. So now we've come full circle and the dimension of Time has been opened. Now it shall be filled with the life that will transform, generation after generation, and eventually humankind will rise and praise the name of Prion.

Meaning/Stage: the domicile of deepest emotion where feeling is paramount

Reversal: a place of apathy, where one no longer feels any passion or purpose

THE ACOLYTE OF WATER
(PAGE OF CUPS)

A prince of ponds named Tacarog, he played in perfect places, by lily pads and smiling faces. Riding his seahorse to and fro, he trumpeted through the sour foam.

The algae trees and stones with moss surround my limpid pool across from which Dolphins play in the river's currents. Frogs and mudskippers flock to the shoals. The gentle sweeping tides relent just long enough for my sandy bed to settle in and go to sleep. But then, what's this? A furry creature leaps across my pond into the woods. A jackrabbit that is rarely seen comes along on in-between days, playing among the pussy willows, reeds and banks of watery meadows. The secret way to the temple of hearts is hidden in my dreams, the most secretive parts.

Meaning/Stage: careful, exquisite and artistic, dramatic, performing for others, playful and unique in your approach, be emotional, intuitive, intimate, loving, but be aware of yourself and willing to explain your expressions in an articulate, passionate manner

Reversal: clumsy, reckless, silly, flirting with disaster, reckless and yet purposeful, flying by the seat of your pants, trusting your feelings to guide you through

The Frog and the Seahorse: Water signs, less evolved form, all properties.

Personality traits: emotional, creative, nurturing, compassionate, imaginative, spiritual, psychic, suspicious, mood, irrational, unpredictable, wishy-washy, dramatic, sensitive, depressive, impractical

Cusp sign: Lepus "The Hare" (Born February 29th)

THE BEARER OF WATER
(KNIGHT OF CUPS)

Ren and Resh, the siblings, often called Diaphanous Fin, were eternally locked in a struggling spin. Some said the battle was raging within, but they were of one mind, not unlike many twins.

> We both contend to be given the choice to speak with the ocean's stentorian voice. So, we each grab a hold of the orb of the soul and neglect all the rest of the world we rule. The river runs rapid and washes us away into watery oblivion where we shall remain. Forever engaged in a battle for truth. Every gill blows a bubble. Every scale chips a tooth. When we tire and expire with nothing to give, in our unconscious dreams we will still not forgive. It's the curse of duality born in our brains. The river had stolen all we've worked to obtain. Nothing will change and what little remains will be left as a mystery, never explained.

Meaning/Stage: regal, pleasing, gallant, graceful, saintly, pure, expose yourself to the world, show everyone exactly who you are, romantic, imaginative, sensitive, refined, introspective, others want you to show them your true self, open yourself up and be willing to share yourself

Reversal: overemotional, fanciful, temperamental, over-refined, overbearing, boastful, rude, overstepping your boundaries, too much attention paid to making yourself into what others want you to be, attention starved, time to be more reserved and introverted

Pisces "The Fish"
(Born February 19th-March 20th)

Personality traits: intuitive, artistic, versatile, absorbing, loyal, homebody, generous, kind, receptive, appreciative, understanding, instinctual, compassionate, self-sacrificing, calm, faithful, loving, tenderhearted, spiritual, rebellious, unconventional, draining, emotive, unreliable, idle, careless, impractical, ineffective, fickle, indiscreet, gullible, pessimistic, fearful, melancholy

Cusp sign: Eridanus "The River"
(Born March 16th-March 24th)
Bearer of Vapor, Mutable Property.

THE KEEPER OF WATER
(QUEEN OF CUPS)

Gatricus, born of the star fragmented, had a needle for a tail upon which poison fermented.

With claws to snap a stone in twain and make a mud puddle of your brain, a swimming flame, I guard the passageways into the underworld. My noble squire is a purple swan who wears a crown and sings a song while playing ivory lyre strings. Vibrations call, like sirens, bringing the ears of wanton sailors hence. They fall to their knees and they repent, but mercy is not an inborn trait, and those who enter don't escape. A creeping chill runs down my back as my stinging tail is arched to crack. Provoke my wrath and you will die. I rest. In wait, I silently lie. Once burned was I by the angry sun, so I crawled deep into a watery hole. I tunnel so far into the world below that now the subterranean is my home. The salty oceans cool my shell. I am fire underwater, even hotter than Hell.

Meaning/Stage: accept and give someone their due, compassion, understanding, empathy, wisdom gained from experience, calm, diplomatic, caring, tolerant, thoughtful and empathetic, someone who works to help you discover your true feelings, wise counsel

Reversal: writing others off, disassociation, disconnected, passionless, careless and an utter lack of compassion, unable to connect with someone else, numb

Scorpio "the Scorpion"
(October 23rd-November 21st)

Personality traits: imaginative, intuitive, critical perception, analytical, fast healers, profound, serious mind, charming, social, hard-working, helpful, strong-willed, motivated, passionate, resourceful, aware, sexual, grounded, practical, violent, jealous, resentful, distrusting, secretive, temperamental, detached, overly sensitive, suspicious, prideful

Cusp sign: Lyra "The Lyre"
(Born November 17th -November 25th)
Keeper of Vapor, Fixed Property.

THE MASTER OF WATER
(KING OF CUPS)

Arellion, the harbinger of changing tides, she was the queen of the oceans and rivers beside.

Leviathans tremble whenever I move. The cold quiet ocean will change with my mood. From a massive tsunami to a small, summer storm, all the sea life surrenders when my form comes ashore. My scepter and crown are controlling the tides in the wake of emotions the hydra will rise and powerful titans will clash 'neath the stars, and the waters will drown out the cries from afar. Anchors descend and the trenches are torn. The waters flow freely. The planet is born. All that you feel, when you leap or you swoon, is controlled by myself and the power of the Moon. Meridians parallel, tropics and tides, the bend of the Earth twixt the waters and sky can be seen with my heart and an explorer's eye. I've a shell that is crusty, created to hide my soft, swollen heart that is beating inside. The power of passion, love and hate, anger, joy and other states are drops of rain in the endless sea. Emotions will trap you and then set you free.

Meaning/Stage: an affectionate embrace, deeper connections, embracing, show others that you love them, be generous, tenderhearted, intuitive, psychic, spiritual, freely express and give of the love you have, show others how you feel and don't be shy about it

Reversal: conceited, elitist, self-serving, cold, selfish, you need to recognize these things about yourself or you will end up lonely and disregarded

Cancer "The Crab"
(Born June 21ˢᵗ-July 22ⁿᵈ)

Personality traits: emotional, nostalgic, tenacious, purposeful, energetic, wise, philosophical, dramatic, artistic, imaginative, difficult to anticipate, perplexing, nurturing, understanding, protective, devious, self-pitying, impulsive, over-emotional, inferiority complex, stubborn conviction, contradictory, self-deprecating, naïve, moody, clingy, manipulative, insecure

Cusp sign: Hydra "The Water Serpent"
(Born July 18ᵗʰ-July 26ᵗʰ)
Master of Vapor, Cardinal Pproperty.

Thus ends the tale of Eon and Iode. But the adventure continues! The next chapter tells the tale of the elemental guardians brought into being by dark magic. They waged war across the planet until a truce was formed and they were charged with rearing the grandchildren of the universe.

CHAPTER 6
THE DIFFUSION
"PAUSE"

BEYOND ETERNITY

We have passed through the final membrane, into the infinite beyond all that is, was and will ever be. Here we communed with Prion, and all that occurred in the Space between Time was revealed.

Meaning/Stage: awe and enlightenment, that which can only be understood through meditation, or the passage of the soul into another plane, the peace that passeth understanding

Reversal: complete and utter darkness, obliteration, non-existence

AMALGAMATION

AsTaroth, a general of the Shadow Queen's armada, created a cauldron for transforming Prion's essence and for manipulating the seasons. With his cunning and evil will, he created avatars of the elements in an attempt to unseat the newborn archons of Eon and Iode and claim their power for Nema.

Meaning/Stage: the will to perform evil acts and subvert the work of others, putrification of the pure, artifice, seeking to destroy and use the power of others to bring about their downfall, stealing fire from the gods, defamation

Reversal: toying with powers you can't comprehend, misuse, the ends do not justify the means, the road to hell is paved with good intentions

EVAPORATION

AsTaroth lured the Phoenix and the Salamander to the ocean temple's shore, but the Tortoise and the Undine were prepared to withstand the war. Each time a battled ensued the planet bore the brunt. AsTaroth cackled with delight, watching the furies he'd unleashed clash and mar the Earth Mother.

Meaning/Stage: tempers flare and are extinguished by emotional responses, anger and frustration, saying things you might not mean in the heat of the moment, an unrestrained and somewhat embarrassing emotional outpouring as a result of personal insults or injuries.

Reversal: a hot-button issue is diffused by empathy and a feeling that you may need to be more compassionate and considerate of the feelings of others, admit you were wrong and apologize

PRECIPITATION

Then, in the wake of the first battle, AsTaroth sent the Sky Dragon and his Sylph to blindside the great Tortoise. The Undine was knocked down by the powerful winds and the Dragon's lightning breath and thunderous tail.

Meaning/Stage: out of control, furious argument, there is no longer a separation between belief and feeling, words become weapons, attachments to stubborn ideals stir the emotions and create feuds that cannot be resolved until one or the other relents

Reversal: your feelings of respect and love for another allow you to agree to disagree, to let go and diffuse a potentially virulent situation before it grows beyond your control

EROSION

The Tortoise and the Undine then retreated towards the mountains. They wore away the rocks to erode the power of Earth's protectors. The imbalance of energies shifted and the Earth Mother was changed yet again. AsTaroth tightened his grip as the wild power of the furies threatened to break away from his mastery.

Meaning/Stage: no ground to stand on, your foundation is disappearing, everything you've built is being taken away before your eyes, time to defend yourself and cut your losses, a lack of preparation, a surprise attack of emotions that utterly decimates you and leaves you with a sinking feeling, watching it all slip away

Reversal: Helping to foster the growth of another without being asked. Perhaps you should not help though, for some things need to be learned individually

CONGESTION

Meanwhile, locked in deadly combat in the sky, the other furies made their battle. The Phoenix and the Dragon were the Spirit and the Mind, fighting over who should rule the planet. All the while, AsTaroth was losing his power to influence these furies. They were growing beyond his control.

Meaning/Stage: the urge to act versus the perceived consequences, playing the devil's advocate, creating friction because you are not willing to blindly follow or jump onboard a ship that has not been proven seaworthy, creating a smoke screen so you can escape, engaging in an argument that makes you look like you are trying to create tension, when in reality- you are just being cautious, not willing to abandon logic for the sake of blind impulse, focusing on the details and not the big picture

Reversal: inspiration and collaboration that leads to furious action, impassioned efforts, a project that seems to immediately thrive because both parties are deeply engaged and invested in its success

DETERIORATION

The Earth was scorched by fire when the Phoenix woke from sleep. But the Tiger did not fear him. She attacked with claws and teeth. All the while AsTaroth sat watching things transpire. The chaos he'd created was beginning to expire.

Meaning/Stage: no matter what you do, everything seems to fall apart, inability to stabilize, waste, all of your resources are being used up, nothing left to offer, trying too hard, burning out, leaving behind a trail of devastation, nothing can be salvaged

Reversal: success but not without loss, burning bridges, using something until it is completely gone and then moving on to the next thing, leaving nothing for the next person in line

RELOCATION

The Dragon came calling, but his power was diminished, and the Sylph attacked but could not penetrate the wall of solid matter. AsTaroth then realized, just as all the furies had, that the unwinable war was ending and an accord would soon be reached. Prion's will prevailed and Nema's scourge had been thwarted from within.

Meaning/Stage: having an unfair advantage without having to try, protection from the words of others, impenetrable skin and an indomitable will, although many will bombard you with questions and accusations, you are unbending and cannot be swayed, there is little you have not heard or considered, hence you become a bastion of your own personal truth

Reversal: allowing the gossip and whisperings of others to create doubt, you know your own mind, but now you are second-guessing yourself and falling prey to the ideals that others are trying to force upon you

INCINERATION

Each unto their own, the four corners they would keep. Surrendering to each other without final victory or defeat. They turned their backs on Time and instead became protectorates. They made a pact to rule as one unto the will of Prion. To the South would be the Temple of Fire where the Phoenix and the Salamander were charged with raising the Alchemist who would one day purify the spirit with the primal essence of being.

Meaning/Stage: BE! the impetus to exist, this is the birth of purpose and a powerful lust for life

Reversal: having no compulsion or desire, a spiritual death

SUFFOCATION

The earthen temple of the Apothecary was a tomb inside a garden, ever growing like an Eden, full of life and so much earthly pleasure. The Dwarf and his White Tiger stood sentry and let none step o'er the Western boundary. They became preservers of all the resting bodies, as they returned unto their mother's womb.

Meaning/Stage: DO! the impetus to act, this is the actuation of a strong and healthy body

Reversal: sickness, weakness, failing to heal, physical death

OBLITERATION

The echo of a primal storm shook the Castle in the Sky. The Scientist could see into the mind of every unblinking, inward eye. No wonder he wouldn't stop crying, for what child could bear such thoughts? The Sylph and her Blue Dragon kept a watchful eye on this wunderkind.

Meaning/Stage: THINK! the impetus to reason, the inception of an idea and the formation of learning and memories

Reversal: thoughtless, empty-headed, stupidity, a psychological death

DILUTION

Protected by the universe, the Philosopher was sound asleep. She dreamt up all the love to fill the ocean's endless deep. The Undine and the Tortoise cradled her and sang her songs. Her heart did beat in tandem with the tide's soft lullaby.

All of the protectors now had purposes. They would serve the will of Prion and to these children of the twin demiurges they would be bound to answer forever after.

Meaning/Stage: FEEL! the impetus to emote and express, the origins of emotions and the expressive nature of mankind

Reversal: loveless, numb, cold, uncaring, an emotional death

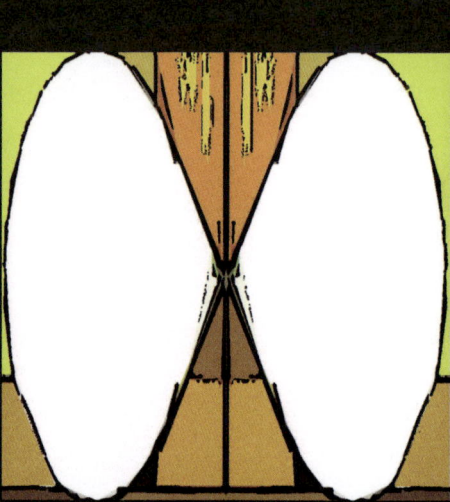

CHAPTER 7
THE TALE OF TIME
"CHANGE"

THE SOURCE AND THE VOID

We begin with no beginning, all that is, was and will ever be, and yet, none of it at all. Only the shadow of what Time itself is exists, at least to us, for we created our own idea of Time. Time is a series of happenings. It started from a point without an origin and blossomed outward until it could stretch no further. Then, it contracted like a recoiling muscle. It shriveled up until it reached the very source from which it sprang and then it tunneled inward imploding until the same process had fulfilled itself a second time. Then it started over again. The shape this process made was that of the lazy eight, an hourglass, or infinity. This is a concept that we, as human beings, cannot possibly hope to ever understand, for our thought process is linear. We see things from a very narrow perspective. We cannot fathom the idea of one line extending in an infinite amount of directions in complete synchronicity, to reconnect with itself infinitely across the vastness of eternity. We cannot wrap our minds around the idea of something we cannot measure or visualize.

The first image and the prelude to the story of "Fledgling" represents this eternal enigma. It symbolizes that which is beyond our scope of reasoning and is not meant to be understood, only acknowledged. It is awe inspiring, humbling, and terrifying. It is everything and nothing, and neither of those ideas, for they were established by humans. This card represents that which is on the outside of that realm of reasoning, the astral plane. We are destined to die in order to truly live. The endless cycle of duality is plunging and breaching perpetually into the infinite endless nothingness and everything that is and never was, all balled into one primal point of fused fury and opposing darkness and light. The skeleton symbolizes Prion (Space) and the progerian baby is Nema (Time).

Meaning/Stage: (birth and death intertwined), eternity, that which cannot be understood, it simply is and is not

Reversal: That which is abundantly clear, it could not be more obvious.

FLEDGLING BEFORE THE PLUNGE
(0 THE FOOL)

This is the story of Fledgling. This is the beginning of destiny. Fledgling was the awakened one. Drawing Eon and Iode's children forth, like moths to the proverbial flame. Fledgling activated their innermost power. Fledgling was special and felt it. Raised as an orphan, never told the tale of the primordial parents from whence all life sprang, Fledgling was the unassuming, chosen one. Prion is reborn once every thousand years when the spirit of creation is desperately needed. Otherwise, Space remains dormant. Nema is an unpredictable enigma of which very little can be speculated. Iode is reborn in every generation, multiple times every day. Eon is reborn much less often, only a few times every hundred years or so. The powerful Iode is our ethereal grandmother, the mother of the Earth and the Queen of our cosmos, and Eon is our grandfather, father to our Sun and the King of our universe. Fledgling, unaware, secretly the first human avatar of Prion, was sent out into the wild, along with a protective phantom familiar, an animal that could change shape and become any creature that Fledgling desired. Fledgling's legendary task was to climb the daunting, purple mountain and to touch the forbidden fruit of the elusive Crystal Tree that never grew in the same place twice.

Meaning/Stage: innocence, new horizons, independent, intellectual, altruistic, progressive, unpredictable, rebellious, impersonal, eccentric, robust, dynamic, beginning, spontaneity, faith, apparent folly, new phase or path, adventure, the unknown, impulsive, carefree, letting go, believing, first step on a journey, leap of faith, taking chances, eagerness, awkwardness, open-minded, unused talent, ideas, hope, an apprentice, frivolous, laughing, joy, absolute freedom

Reversal: reckless behavior, stagnation due to bad decisions, possible injury, folly, extravagance, mismanagement, intoxication, apathy, vanity, horseplay, trickery

THE ALCHEMIST, APOTHECARY, SCIENTIST and PHILOSOPHER
(I THE MAGICIAN)

Upon reaching and touching the singular, prismatic fruit of the Crystal Tree, Fledgling witnessed the branches coming into bloom for the first time in this dimension. The fruit was actually a key. Fledgling was suddenly swept away into a Space outside of Time and came face to face with the four wise sages. They were the ancient children of Eon and Iode, immortal, though aged beings, all born just before our timeline began. Each would unlock a part of Fledgling's sacred being, just as the prophecy had long foretold. A spirit immortal, a body unbreakable, a mind unlimited and a heart perpetual: these gifts bestowed upon Fledgling by Prion and revealed through the sages in unison, manifested and transformed themselves into magical weapons. The four prime elements harnessed and embodied by these four elemental beings of powerful belief became a wand, a gemstone, a sword and a chalice. From each of them would spring all systems of thought and the endless manipulations of reality. The stars and the seasons were named by them and each of us was born beneath their symbols, which form a secret, unspoken language that everyone understands.

Meaning/Stage: individuality, exacting, studious, methodical, humane, critical, skeptical, picky, sloppy, precise, dignified, congenial, curious, expressive, adaptable, restless, scheming, scattered, talkative, spirited, independent, manifesting thought, action and cultivation, concentration, power, conscious, aware, ability to reach goals, endeavoring to learn and grow

Reversal: greed, ego, abuse of power, mental illness, nothing to work with, utter failure

I have also assigned separate meanings to each type of magician. They are as follows:

The Alchemist: complete cycle, materialization, deeply studied, intellect

Reversal: miscalculation, secrecy, error, failed attempts

The Apothecary: prowess, confidence, uniqueness, otherworldly, gifted

Reversal: corrupt, evasive, unstable, unpredictable

The Scientist: bending things to ones will, presence, depth, power

Reversal: irritability, conceit, abusive, violent

The Philosopher: understanding, creativity, harnessed energy, penetration

Reversal: distracted, lethargic, selfish, suspicious nature

VISION OF THE WHISPERING DREAM
(II THE HIGH PRIESTESS)

After ingesting an elixir made by the sages from the juice contained in the fruit of the Crystal Tree, Fledgling fell into a deep sleep and had a lucid dream of a locked door constructed by and embedded in the fabric of the universe. Using the prismatic key (the plucked fruit's leftover rind), to unlock it, Fledgling crossed the threshold into the astral plane: the realm of Prion, where the river of souls flows from here to there and back again. There, a vision of a whispering dream came forth and showed Fledgling the history of the universe, as well as all the tales of every hero that would "follow in the chosen one's footprints." These innumerable generations would be of Fledgling's bloodline. Fledgling was then revealed to be the first human avatar of the eldest God: Prion. A penetrative voice, unlike any ever heard and yet as familiar as thine own came forth in a whispered tone. All of the under-gods were, there and then, condemned to die by this voice of the highest and most ancient of wills, for they were ungrateful and made unholy that which was designed to be kept sacred. In their stead, mankind would rein, but first, Fledgling would have to defeat these under-gods who lingered in this dimension to torment and enslave all mortals.

Meaning/Stage: mysterious, sensitive, traditional, sympathetic, intuitive, manipulative, pessimistic, kind and benevolent, inactivity, unconscious, awareness, potential, mystery, withdrawn, receptive, patience, passive, imagination, allowing development, recollection, acknowledgement, seeing what is concealed, secrets, the unknown, hidden wisdom, dreams, a vision of what lies beneath, non active, observant, internal, clairvoyance, predestination, protection, encouragement, a beacon, revelations

Reversal: superficiality, it's time to let go, mystery, temporary shelter, possibilities, somebody is plotting against you, there are secrets yet to be uncovered

MY MOTHER'S BLESSING
(III THE EMPRESS)

Upon waking, Fledgling was reborn as an infant in yet another dimension outside of time. This was the remnant realm of Primordea, the elemental substrate out of which emerged the twin demiurges, Eon and Iode. This was a sanctuary and reliquary of memories and slumbering, ancient power. Here, Fledgling would enjoy the fruits of heaven and be raised as a god should have been raised. The Mother of matter would give all the love that could ever be desired. Fledgling would become boundlessly fertile, the progenitor of the tribes of all mankind.

Meaning/Stage: wholeness and contentedness, patience, dependability, practical, conservative, power and influence, exacting, studious, methodical, humane, critical, skeptical, picky, precision, dignity, fertility, abundance, growth, stability, healthy, satisfaction, motherhood, senses, nature, reawakening, birth, nourishing, tenderness, children, pleasure, the body, appreciation of beauty, activity, plants and animals, harmony with the rhythms of the planet, bearing fruit, a gradual progression towards maturity

Reversal: lack, wasted energies, depression, decay, putrification, extinction, a long and torturous decline, anguish, a barren womb, stubborn, possessive, materialistic, sloppy,

MY FATHER'S OATH
(IV THE EMPEROR)

Then, after growing into adolescence, Fledgling would be taken to the halls of the mighty Father of energy. There, all lessons of skill and cunning would be taught and preparations would be made for Fledgling to wage war upon those who would use their powers against the will of Prion. Sternly forced to wield the elemental weapons and hone those skills implicit to becoming a warrior, Fledgling would learn the hard way and it would fire-harden the immortal spirit within. Fledgling's power grew untamed, but was instilled with focus and patience. When the time came, Fledgling passed every test and was granted freedom to take the essence of Prion out into the harsh and unforgiving world.

Meaning/Stage: powerful, competitive, dynamic, impulsive, domineering, intolerant, arrogant, monetary success, authority, logic, responsibility, discipline, foundation, fatherhood, structure, regulation, direction, setting an example, defense, security, explanation, system, order, application, coordination, endurance, stick-to-itiveness

Reversal: lack of character or discipline, weakness, destructive, instability, falling to pieces because of a weak foundation, hasty

THE ORB OF GUIDANCE
(V THE HIEROPHANT)

Fledgling then would travel along a winding road and climb a seemingly endless set of stairs to reach the spiritual master. This servant of God is firmly rooted in the earth and yet reaches far into the depths of the spirit towards the Aethyr and into the mind of Prion. A newfound guide and guru, he would now challenge Fledgling to be sure that the Mother and Father's tests had been satisfactorily passed and that there was true worth in the heart of this, the rising avatar of Prion. Fledgling would be taught of the nature of the earthbound spirit and the soul with all of it's emotions, then shown a vortex through which a soul and spirit might step, entwined, in order to understand what it meant to be what one must become in order to overcome those who would call themselves gods.

Meaning/Stage: saintly, stoic, calm, patience, dependability, practical, conservative, power and influence, tradition, conformity, expanding awareness through spirituality, education, group, identification, study, seeking meaning, ceremonies, rules, discipline, fitting in, commitment, loyalty, a great teacher, the voice of experience

Reversal: non-conformity, unorthodox, pagan, sacrilegious, inattentive, someone who refuses to listen or take the wisdom of others into account, stubborn, willful, possessive, greedy, materialistic

THE CROSSROADS OF CONJUNCTION AND DIVERSION
(VI THE LOVERS)

Fledgling's spirit and soul, as one, were projected into the vault of heaven, where the memory of the first Eden resided. Becoming and reliving the long-passed life of an age-old incarnation of Eon, Fledgling encountered a counterpart, a descendant of Iode, who would be the mother of psyche. She, the bearer of all people, had within her 1,000 wombs, like buds upon the branches of the Crystal Tree, and each would birth a child unto our mortal dimension. These children would proliferate and create the entire race of humankind. In this Space, Fledgling would experience the ultimate affliction, the emotion of romantic love. Physical pleasures abound there in a paradise of the mind. All that Fledgling had been tasked with remembering was designed to be easily forgotten. It was a test of pure resolve. Their perfect love gave birth to nations, but then, she died with an arrow through her heart. Fledgling then met with the greatest of sorrows, and the whispering voice returned. It had come to say that this had all been a dream; an entire lifetime of feelings, and this was the consequence of mortal life. Such is the pain of love and loss. Fledgling was made to know love and to become that love: the love of all the world. But Fledgling could never again be anything close to mortal. "Take pity on them, and love them," the whispering voice implored, "for they will endure this pain generation after generation."

Meaning/Stage: completeness, perfect bliss, congenial, curious, expressive, adaptable, talkative, spirited, independent yet codependent, harmony, love, trust, balance of opposites, sexuality, relationship, marriage, sympathy, opening, philosophy, making a choice, temptation, a symbiosis

Reversal: insecurity, separation, infidelity, communication breakdown, unrequited love, divorce, restless, scheming, scattered,

THE SEVERING CONQUEST
(VII THE CHARIOT)

Fledgling was then made to return to Earth, to lead great armies in battle against the scourge of Time. Nema had made a terrible king and a merciless queen of two unworthy godlings, and they rode rampant, conquering the world in their chariot of death. Fledgling would lead the mortal armies through years of long battles, using the legendary, magical weapons in repeated attempts to slay this goliath pair. After ages upon ages of fighting, when all the armies of the world had been slain, Fledgling finally prevailed, defeating the charioteers in combat. It was an epic battle to the death. Impossibly, the unbreakable Fledgling was wounded by poisoned thorns, sent flying from the blackened hands of Nema's godling servants. Bright orbs of Prion's power had followed and protected our hero. All of the enemy's arrows had broken upon the air, save the one that pierced to the heart. Wounded, Fledgling took up the reins of the bloody chariot and rode it unto the gates of heaven where the spirit and the soul were divided; only to be rejoined anew and reconceived in the womb of the same dream from whence sprouted perfect love.

Meaning/Stage: conquest, kind, benevolence, sensitive, traditional, sympathetic, intuitive, victory, control, effort, passion, overcoming adversity, will, self-assertion, goals, competition, determination, concentration, focus, identifying obstacles, self-confidence, faith in oneself, steady, maintenance, mastery, momentum, collision course

Reversal: out of control, inner conflict, overwhelmed by circumstances, inability to advance, becoming trapped, an inescapable situation, being torn in two directions, regression, potential energy squandered, pessimistic, manipulative, lazy, selfish

THE UNTAMABLE CORE
(VIII STRENGTH)

Although Fledgling's time on Earth was not yet over, the plane of Primordea would become home for what seemed like a thousand lifetimes. During this time without time, Fledgling reborn, would inhabit a primeval, celestial body, one of great virtue and strength, previously not but an effigy asleep in lifeless stone. Adorned with the countenance of the first offspring of the mother of psyche, a spirit exuding sensuous energy and nearly limitless power, even the proud lions of the eternal garden would bow before Fledgling now and vortices of the ethereal poured omnipotence into Fledgling's soul from beyond the impenetrable iron gates. Being thusly imbued with a perfect power to be and to understand all aspects of the universe, to recognize the interchangeability of energy and matter, to remember the eventual fates of those who had not yet been born and to impel them towards their destinies, Fledgling danced and radiated the absolute essence of Prion. Watching from behind the veil between planes as the spirits of the deceased returned to the primordial core of God, Fledgling saw the souls of the universe slipping into the silver river of the unconscious where they would each find their own heaven, for the mind, being the basis of perceived reality, makes any soul's dream as true and as real as the corporeal. The only truth that exists is that of the perception of an individual consciousness through the eyes of Prion. There is no absolute truth but God. As our hero waits, embodying virtue, the world changes.

Meaning/Stage: firm, energetic, optimism, creativity, generosity, pride, clever, ingenious, divine force, power, patience, gentility, love, self control, endurance, spirit, resolve, acceptance, calm, tolerant, kindness, persuasion, amassing power, gathering energies

Reversal: abuse of power, weakness, lack of faith and integrity, taking it lying down, becoming complacent, taking something for granted, letting an opportunity pass you by refusing to be told what to do, over-bearing, cruel, pretentious, boastful

THE NOMAD AND HIS INEXTINGUISHABLE LANTERN
(IX THE HERMIT)

After much timelessness had passed, Fledgling was unexpectedly reunited with a physical body and returned to the planet Earth. Following the glinting of a distant light at the end of an exhaustive tunnel, Fledgling emerged from the spatial dimensions outside of time. There, at the very core of our planet, Fledgling passed through the "Orbiculus Ocularis," (mirror of the universe) and reentered the temporal realm. Still aglow with an otherworldly light, Fledgling sat down and fell into a sleep-like, regenerative meditation. The mirror of the universe was preceded by an ancient, reflective altar, made of the same multi-faceted material as the crystal tree, which Fledgling named "the Gazing Chamber." As our hero stared into the altar, all of the stories of the entire universe, hidden behind ancient eyes, came forth and were reflected therein. This place was designed to be a temple that would become home to those who would one day swear to guard the gate that led directly into the essential mind of Prion. Upon waking, Fledgling realized this new body was aged and weak. However, Fledgling's mind was still aflame with the secret knowledge of Prion. Being disposed to isolate and hide this divine knowledge from the world, Fledgling dwelled within the deep Earth for an age, all the while navigating the subterranean labyrinths that had hidden the ancient temple from any who would ever try to find it. Something stirred in the shadows, unbeknownst to Fledgling. Happening upon a cave that finally led to the overworld, Fledgling found a new home in the desperate wastelands. It was there that our wise and experienced hero reflected, fasted and wrote down all of the divine knowledge that could be comprehended by a mortal mind. These writings would become the ideals of living existence known to the Aggregates as "Fledgling's Axioms."

Meaning/Stage: lonely, reflective, exacting, studious, methodical, humane, critical, skeptical, picky, introversion, soul seeking, a search for illumination, introspection, solitude, silence, wise council, withdrawing, retreat, solitary confinement

Reversal: resistance, mania, ego gets in the way of good sense, social life, you need to get out more, you have become too introverted, social anxiety

THE FLICKERING RIDDLE OF FATE
(X THE WHEEL OF FORTUNE)

A surreptitious villain stepped forth from the darkness, a servant of Time's shadow, and challenged Fledgling's power. Fledgling's mortal coil was easily sundered, and Nema's acolyte knew it was advantageous to attack our hero in this weakened form. But then, to Fledgling's rescue came a band of mythic creatures: three sorceresses, distant daughters of Iode, and Eon's newest son, a centaur archer known as Prince Kyrn, who was a healer with great powers of the sun and the rain clouds. Great, great grandchild of the ancient centaur, Acha, who displayed supernatural skill beyond any who wielded a bow, Kyrn had been convinced by visions and a whispering voice in his dreams that he was needed. He followed his visions and found himself journeying into the wastelands beside a triune of magical sisters. Together, this band of travelers defeated the shadow assassin and cast a protective spell around Fledgling's mortal form, allowing it to change its shape. Then the hand of ancient Eon came forth from Kyrn's spirit and spun a wheel of fire about the three devout daughters of Iode, opening a gate that revealed the riddle of Fledgling's fate. The world of man had fallen into chaos after the great wars, so very long ago. Fledgling now realized that the responsibility to set things right would fall on the shoulders of Prion's avatar. The absence of Prion's will in the material plane had given Nema a foothold to corrupt it. A decision would have to be made.

Meaning/Stage: unpredictable, enthusiasm, generosity, religious, philosophical, augmentative, tenacious, diligent, change, innumerable possibilities, connections, turning point, movement, personal vision, luck, fate, miracles, surprises, getting involved, discovery, expansion, gaining a greater perspective of things, perpetuity, the wheel keeps turning, if you don't get out of its way- you might get flattened!

Reversal: loss of fortunes, blunt, impatient, pushy, passage of time, the unknown, now is not the time to leave things up to fate, take a step back, cease and desist, there is a piece missing from the puzzle

THE BALANCE AND THE HAMMERSTROKE
(XI JUSTICE)

Full of righteous indignation, and now empowered with the ability to change shape, Fledgling returned to the world of men in disguise. Carrying the sword of ultimate truth, with which to pierce the veil of lies that had been obscuring mankind's vision, Fledgling sought to bring swift judgment to bear in the form of a blind oracle. It was a necessary deception, this hypocrisy with good intentions. The ends would justify the means. At least for now, that's how it seemed. All who saw Fledgling's familiar visage were inspired to follow. The blind oracle spoke of what was right and just. They believed that this representative of virtue had come to release them from bondage and restore the balance. Their hearts became light, as the anger they'd been harboring for generations was reconciled. Upon entering the unified kingdom which had been formed by the assimilation of all peoples under one banner, Fledgling saw that there was order, but at the expense of freedom. Finding a terrible queen ruling as a tyrant on high, sitting on a throne of harsh prejudice, committing terrible atrocities of which we cannot speak, Fledgling took away her power with Prion's will and dealt to her a deathly blow. It was reciprocity for the love of all those who had been wronged, yet remained faithful.

Meaning/Stage: moderating, neutral, cooperation, diplomacy, persuasion, sociable, decisive, judgmental, just and noble, equity, justice, reason, truth, purity, compromise, decision, cause and effect, responsibility, impartiality, distinguishing between right and wrong

Reversal: bias, injustice, bigotry, prejudice, narrow-minded, a skewed perspective, unfair, imbalanced, hypocritical, fickle

THE ACCEPTANCE OF THE MARTYR
(XII THE HANGED MAN)

As Fledgling executed the tyrant, releasing a hidden shadow of evil from it's stolen, corporeal form, that very darkness, one of Nema's slaves, attached itself to Fledgling's skin and used the shape-shifting spell to create an evil visage. All were taken aback by Fledgling's changed appearance. Many who were once grateful were now convinced that their savior had been spreading lies. They felt betrayed and said that Fledgling was evil, manipulating them to gain their faith, only to rule over them. They said what Fledgling preached was NOT the will of God, and so they persecuted and tortured our hero in indescribable ways. Fledgling was hung upside down and drowned in a lake of tears after being made a spectacle. There were twelve who mourned, however, despite the deception, for they had come to love and believe in Fledgling. They tried to stop the others from jumping to conclusions, from making a horrible mistake, but they did not have the power of persuasion to stop the angry mob. Through Fledgling's willful sacrifice, those who kept their faith in Prion soon realized that they too had divine abilities. It was during this time, following the dismantling of the unified kingdom, that the Order of the Ecliptic was founded. The most faithful perceived the secrets of the universe, for Prion whispered unto them. This secret society would persist for all time, as protectors of the Earth against the dark forces of Time's shadow and Her spawn.

Meaning/Stage: solemn, depressed, compassion, introspection, artistic, dreamy, timid, impractical, escapist, melancholy, tender and harmonious, self-sacrifice, piercing the veil of perception, release, reversal, end of struggle, vulnerable, acceptance, changing ones mind, suspending action, putting others first, surrendering to ones fate

Reversal: attachment, bondage, imprisoned spirit, being outspoken, protesting, dragged away- kicking and screaming, resisting arrest, denial

THE TRANSFORMATION WITHIN THE CHRYSALIS
(XIII DEATH)

Now, having experienced most all that one could in a human life both as a male and as a female, Fledgling was ushered forth on the ancient wings of death to learn the final experience of mortality. Infected with the disease of Time, Fledgling's spirit was ejected from the corporeal shell and the temporal dimension, escaping Nema's grasp to enter, once more, into the mind of Prion. In death Fledgling was again reborn, and simultaneously left behind both a female attribution of matter and a male attribution of energy. Fledgling's spirit spun a silvery, translucent cocoon. It was a celestial chrysalis that would incubate Fledgling's soul, refining it so that all of the remnants of mortality were dissolved and all that remained was divinity. Fledgling ripped open the chrysalis and flicked dry a pair of perfect wings. Death was thereby negated. Fledgling was now one among the gods. Shaking free from mortal dreams and awakening in the Aethyr, Fledgling was suddenly surrounded by undergods and the Nemite horde, locked in chaotic, cosmic combat. Death had been a transient respite and now, rebuilt to resurrect, our hero would have to defend an immortal soul while attempting to rejoin with the displaced spirit that was now up for grabs, drifting through the timelessness of Space. Pushing past all of the undergods and devils, battling over who would claim the rampant spirit for their own, Fledgling was about to recapture it, when a swift and strange angel caught up with it first. So, Fledgling pursued this angel as she retreated with her prize, across the river of souls.

Meaning/Stage: sorrowful, anguish, recollecting, motivation, resourceful, investigative, passionate, vengeful, temperamental, sarcastic, suspicious, down to earth, generous, transformation, rebirth, transition, abrupt change in flow, ending, elimination, completion, parting ways, set adrift, in-between, essentials, back to basics, starting over, turning over a new leaf, caught in the path of a sweeping change, fate, the unavoidable

Reversal: inertia, slow change, painful metamorphosis, death, decay, running out of time, finality, oblivion

THE COHESION OF EQUILIBRIUM
(XIV TEMPERANCE)

The strange angel noticed that Fledgling was following her and so she turned and said: "Come with me and I will show you the way back." Together they escaped the Aethyr and crossed the river of souls into the Elysium Corridor. It was a place of perfect balance and temperate storms. Everything moved in circles and maintained a cohesive equilibrium. There, among the elements prime, the angel gave back to Fledgling the precious, immortal spirit she had captured. Whole once more, our hero felt all the powers of the universe surge and envelop the spirit, the body, the soul and the heart, as they were once more reunited. "Who are you?" our hero asked, but the angel had no answer. "Here, I am what I am," she said, "…but there," she pointed to the distant Earth "I am something else entirely. If you follow the river backwards it will lead you to the temporal gate." Although the angel resisted, Fledgling insisted that she come along. Hand in hand, a balanced pair, they navigated the planes and approached the corporeal dimension.

Meaning/Stage: peaceful, reflective, forgiving, moderation, patience, balance, maintenance, health, compromise, agreement, harmony, cooperation, healing, recovery, flourishing, gathering, consolidation, synthesis

Reversal: discord, excess, a time to reassess and recover energies, going overboard, taking things too seriously, inability to maintain

THE DRAGON LAYING WASTE
(XV THE DEVIL)

They both came back to Earth and found it in utter ruin. They walked across the scorched ground, destroying Nemites and saving helpless humans from a foul beast's fetid, blackened jaws. It didn't matter though, for all the ones they'd rescued died from fear and despair. Returning to the site of the old cave, where the axioms had been written, and retracing the path that led, deep down, to the temple of the Gazing Chamber, Fledgling found the faithful followers of Prion, bound and being drained of their newly realized powers. Our hero set them free! Then, Fledgling strode into the inner sanctum to find a great dragon and it's keeper. They were laughing. They had been waiting. Chained to the floor were the memories of Fledgling's greatest love. Reminded of the pain, it all came rushing back like water.

Fledgling turned to look at the angel companion, whose face now briefly resembled his love, and then it warped as she changed, into a Nemite demon. She had been a dark, deceptive dream. She'd been used to lure Fledgling here. The true angel had been captured and corrupted against her will. Fledgling had to set her soul free. So in an epic battle Fledgling cast her down, and cut off her wings, then engaged in battle with and smote the massive dragon. So exhausted afterwards, Fledgling was unable to defend the chamber against the powerful keeper of the dragon. He was a plague called Abaddon who sought to absorb our hero's divine essence into himself, for he was one of the many higher order shadows, who commanded a thousand thralls of Nema.

Meaning/Stage: evil, deceitful, responsible, cautious, scrupulous, serious, unforgiving, inhibited, cold, fatalistic, hardworking, stable, material attachment, spiritual bondage, dissatisfaction, addiction, over-indulgence, ignorance, obsession, limitation, despair, doubt, abusive, self-destruction, repression

Reversal: a release, seeing through illusions, understanding and freedom, breaking free from previous paradigms, uninhibited, letting it all hang out, doing what you've always wanted to do, guiltless pleasure

THE TREMORS OF THE STRICKEN TOWER
(XVI THE TOWER)

After falling under Abaddon's sword, Fledgling was cast into the impenetrable tower; a dungeon, like the mouth of hell, where our gallant hero was expected to remain for all time, or until the destroyer of worlds came to consume Earth. But no, Fledgling would escape! Calling upon divine power to release all of Prion's followers who were trapped there alongside, there came a peal of thunder! The destructive power of God was Fledgling's weapon. It arrived in the form of the ancient archon: Ammramm the destroyer! A battle ensued the likes of which none had ever seen. Leviathan and Behemoth clashed in a calamitous "KABOOM!" The mouth of hell, Nema's fiendish grin, which had come to finally devour our hero and end the line of Man, was repelled by the power of Prion. Fledgling had prevailed. The abyssal mouth disappeared and the imprisoned Aggregates of the Ecliptic were released from their infernal bonds. The world began to grow anew and all was set right. The aggregates were reawakened to their powers and many prophecies of the incarnations of Eon and Iode that would follow were professed. Then, ascending from our plane once more, having used the power of Prion instilled within, our hero's mortality began to disintegrate. Fledgling became a being of pure Aethyr. The remnant essence began to coalesce and a new crystal tree sprouted and bore fresh fruit. Each fruit took on the multi-faceted shape of a dodecahedron. If a mortal were to eat it, it would kill them, but they would, in that instant before death, come to know all that there was ever to know. Upon Fledgling's words the Aggregates rebuilt the temples and brought back into being, through magical reincarnation, the ancient Archons. They would inspire humankind and deliver unto the world Fledgling's laws.

Meaning/Stage: chaotic, terrifying, competitive, dynamic, impulsive, power, motivation, resourcefulness, investigative, passionate, vengeful, temperamental, disruption, upheaval, crumbling, eclipse, rapid change, downfall, revelation, release, crisis, eruption, being humbled, suffering, realization, cataclysm

Reversal: entrapment, imprisonment, all things pass in time, eclipse, fall from grace, annihilation, apocalypse

THE WELL OF THE FALLEN WISHING STAR
(XVII THE STAR)

Ascending into the realm of the stars, Fledgling was reunited with the memory of perfect love, drifting through the Aethyr. The soul was intact, but the immortal spirit had become one with Prion. Fledgling united with and embodied love and henceforth was always within. Their minds were joined and their thoughts and hearts became one. Fledgling was swiftly filled with an indomitable swell of hope for humankind. There and then, a new, sacred prophecy was born that would remain a secret, even to the stars, for a millennium. As their perfect love united them, it took shape and merged with all the gratitude and love of humankind. It coalesced into a new form of life, the ethereal child Astrid, whose essence was immediately drawn into the depths of the timeless cosmos and surrounded by the love and power of Prion. Here she would remain, in ageless stasis until called upon. This would be Prion's final avatar who would one day be reborn and renamed on Earth. It would be her destiny to inspire hope and to save the universe from despair and ultimate destruction.

Meaning/Stage: fantastical, enchanting, independent, intellectual, altruistic, progressive, unpredictable, rebellious, eccentric, hope, inspiration, optimism, possibilities, realization of dreams, serenity, generosity, faith, the way is clear, peace, tranquility, harmony, faith in what is yet to come, a positive outlook

Reversal: disappointment, pessimism, unfulfilled hopes and desires, imbalance, clouded vision, blind leading the blind, listen to your inner voice, alone in the dark

ENTROPY OF LUNA
(XVIII THE MOON)

Then unto the Moon our hero was conveyed to solve a great mystery for the gods of the Aethyr. Fledgling would have to find the soul of one who had been trapped therein. It was this soul's essence that had been transformed into the strange, deceptive angel who'd been forced to lure Fledgling back to Earth and into the anxiously awaiting clutches of Abaddon. If our hero could find and emancipate this soul, then the Moon would be free of Nema's temporal spell. This adventure would take many ages and there was much that happened in that time and place. Transitions of slow change and patience were required to unravel the spells that imprisoned it there. Eventually, the soul was found and released, but chose to remain there as a guardian of the lunar throne. The Moon was then of a beneficent nature for a time, a motherly goddess, who provided light in dark times. But this did not last. Eventually, Nema's essence overtook the Moon once more, and it became a harbinger of shadow, orbiting the Earth and drowning all who lived there in an ocean of time. For every complete circle the Moon made around the Earth, Nema's essence expanded and her influence augmented. A shadow of her power usurped the lunar throne and drove men mad, glaring down upon them from the darkened sky.

Meaning/Stage: changing, ponderous, moody, compassion, introspection, artistic, dreamy, timid, illusion, phases, cycles, don't be deceived by outward appearances, apprehension, phobia, anxiety, self deception, vivid dreams or visions, bizarre, loosing purpose, confusion, aimless, disorientation, lost, a time of slow and uncomfortable change

Reversal: recognizing deception before any damage can be done, you are well aware of what is going on, nothing gets past you, allowing events to unfold without worry, you've got an ace in the hole

RADIANCE OF SOLA
(XIX THE SUN)

To be purified forever lasting, Fledgling then passed through the Sun, reliving the purest of all childhoods, filled to bursting with resplendent joy, and becoming a god of the highest order. Joining all at once with a pantheon of powerful, ethereal beings set upon defeating the shadow of Time and bringing about a new order and age of the cosmos, Fledgling raised all of their hands in glory. These ethereal gods bowed before our hero and crowned Fledgling their superior, an essential figurehead who would thenceforth communicate with the core of Prion and shine down the radiant will of the universe. Each time the Moon's face was forced to reflect the distant splendor of the Sun, a little bit of Nema's shadow was burned into oblivion.

Meaning/Stage: happiness, glee, optimism, creativity, generosity, pride, boastful, clever, ingenious, attainment, opportunity, joy, enlightenment, greatness, vitality, assurance, understanding, insight, breakthrough, energized, brilliance, center of attention, health, success, trust, vim and vigor

Reversal: unhappiness, poverty, gloom, but eventually the sun will shine through, positive attitude is obscured by circumstance, joy is fleeting, distracted by inconvenience, don't sweat the small stuff

THE DAY OF RECKONING AND REDEMPTION
(XX JUDGMENT)

When the day of the gods finally came and final judgment fell upon every planet in every galaxy, there would be a battle unlike any have ever known. An inter-stellar war was waged across all dimensions, and Fledgling would be an angelic general and lead the charge towards victory. All who had died and been enveloped by shadow would be called back to life to fight, and the timeless age would end with the slate being wiped clean. The shadow of Time, slept just as Prion had, and awaited the chance to be reawakened. Then, after all was said and done, the gods returned to their source, and all would begin again, for the cycle does not end. It is designed to self-perpetuate forever. Space imploded and ignited, then expanded beyond reason once more. Time slowly crept back into the dimension of existence and new heroes were needed to bring light to pierce the ever-encroaching shadow. The first followers of Prion were remade and given the power to enter into our dimension of Time and to interact with the developing civilizations. They would be observers and protectors who would make contact with the avatars of Eon and Iode who were born to seed the Earth and to remake the essence of humankind, pure and new. Our generation was born of gods, much like Fledgling was reborn. However, the gods of our dimension are but echoes of the gods from previous ages. Time is eternal and the untold ages of the Earth and it's multifaceted dimensions go deeper than any of us realize or can ever know. Our reality is a new beginning for humankind. With each rebirth mortals became more and more individualized and distant from the essence of Prion. We've grown apart from our divine ancestors and become the gods of our own realities. History played out in a much different manner each time the universe reset itself. The gods took less and less interest with each incarnation, returning to their source more readily and leaving any hope of control behind. All except for one deserted us, Nema, the shadow of Time, who would always persist, who would always devour. Even in defeat Time always returns and can traverse limitless dimensions as easily as one can pass from one room to another. Some doors are locked, but they can still be opened with the proper key. Time is always waiting, collecting and preparing to eat the avatars as they are born. Yet there is always hope! Prion watches from afar and responds to those who ask for help. If thou art worthy, you will be saved. And so it was to always be a secret, and remains an enigma to this day.

Meaning/Stage: forgiveness, climax, motivation, resourcefulness, investigative, passionate, vengeful, atonement, forgiveness, self-analysis, renewal, rebirth, absolution, taking a stand, conviction, waking up, making a difference, a new direction, cleansed, refreshed, unburdened, clean slate, a powerful revelation

Reversal: indecision, denial, damnation, purgation is required, passivity, being a push-over, defeatist attitude, giving up

THE ENDLESS HALL OF LIMITLESS DOORS
(XXI THE WORLD)

Blessed to return to the source, Fledgling's soul was finally released into the silvery river of heaven. Now in our hero's divine state, the choice was made to split apart infinitely in order to become like God and enter into the entirety of existence and all of its intricacies, from a single grain of sand, to the life of a fly on the wall, from the eruption of a volcano to a dragon soaring through a thunderstorm, and every moment of every memory of every human who had ever or would ever live. Fledgling's essence would endlessly pass through eternity, being born and reborn again and again. Eventually, it would manifest and be made aware of itself and remember all that it had learned when it first touched the crystal tree so very long ago, and yet it was only yesterday. In a time of great need, our protector would be there, to join with the avatars of

Eon and Iode and defend those who are unable to defend themselves against the scourge of Time. All of these events that have transpired occurred in dreams parallel to our own dimension of perception. These dreams continually bleed into our own realities and evolve into the events of our histories. Gods and men alike are reborn as though they never were, and yet, deep down, there are memories of previous lives waiting to be remembered. Most never recall these memories until after they've died. Most do not realize that their spirits are not their own, only their souls remain undivided and individualized. Even after joining with the river of heaven, and all the voices are made to sing together in joyful chorus, each voice and mind is still infused with it's lifetimes, it's memories, and through them is blessed to create it's own version of heaven and live there for all time beyond time. The spirit of all life and all existence belongs to God and therefore to us all.

Meaning/Stage: open-ended, limitless, synthesis, triumph, endeavors, universal consciousness, integration, involvement, fulfillment, wholeness, combining efforts, unity, accomplishment, blessings, starting over, coming full-circle, beginning of a new life, completion of a grand project

Reversal: imperfection, fear, hesitation, unfinished business, confinement, quarantine, time to perform a diagnostic, root out the problem, reboot the system, stagnation, unwillingness or inability to change

USAGE

Life is perpetual, cyclical, and recurrent, just like the Tarot. Before we begin to play, I want to briefly explain to you the manner in which I approach the Tarot as a tool.

Generally, when I perform a reading, I try to offer perspective on current situations and reveal repeating patterns in our behaviors in order to better pinpoint ways of recognizing the great, unspoken language of the universe. I have a deep reverence for symbolism, even beyond the confines of the traditional Tarot mechanism. I am an artist, and as an artist, symbolism is of paramount importance to me whenever I am trying to express an idea that cannot be put into words. Symbols are the closest thing to proof that we, as humans, share a kind of collective consciousness. Some things simply cannot be expressed verbally. So, we must instead use visual representations of them in the hopes that they will be successful in conveying our intentions. I believe in all things symbolic in this world. All the myths, all the religions and all human efforts towards creating metaphors are reducible to basic archetypes. The Tarot is an illustrated inventory of these icons of human existence. There is an immediate recognition with each image. Whatever it makes you think and feel in that moment is precisely what it means. The more often you look at it though, the more complex its meaning becomes. This is the eternal flux of the spirit of symbolism.

The effigies of the wise old man, the stern but fair king, the beautiful and ethereal priestess, are all very important. These icons help us to define and give faces to what we are trying to communicate. Using these personified ideas in conjunction with other symbols helps to relate a complete thought, if not several, to the viewer. The Tarot's symbolism is usually based on the theme of "the path." This is just a metaphor for the entire experience of one's life. It includes all of the obstacles, triumphs, and failures one faces in a lifetime.

Now, of course it is not possible to have a card that represents every possible condition or occurrence, but the really important stuff is all there. If it's not immediately apparent, then there is at least one card that can be related to the idea you think is missing in some way. You just have to search for it. This is the beautiful thing about the Tarot: it is formless until you, an individual, wraps your imagination around it. Only then does it activate and take shape. The deeper one delves into the language of symbols, the more apparent it becomes that everything is interconnected.

I believe the symbolism inherent in the Tarot is very flexible and can mean extremely different things for each person. I define each card based not only on the widely accepted meaning, but also the immediate personal associations and the way in which the meaning might be stretched to accommodate a specific area of inquiry. I have used the Tarot for self-analysis, daily divination, brainstorming, creative exercises in music and art, and therapy sessions for people who simply need to reestablish their own understanding of where they are in life. The Tarot can be any or all of these things for you.

I hope that after reading this book, you will have established a basic notion of how it speaks to you and what you would like to glean from its wisdom. The Tarot cards can be used beyond the parlor game and the divinatory applications. Being that they are extremely psychological by nature, there are endless possibilities when we begin to attach detailed, personal meanings to them.

This is why I suggest "imprinting" a deck if it is to be your personal deck for reading. When I say imprinting, I am speaking about something similar to the way a musician "breaks in" a new instrument. Eventually the "action" of that instrument will react specifically to your touch, to the notes you play the most and perhaps to the style of music you specialize in. The amount and frequency of pressure you apply to certain strings or keys will loosen them more than the others, effectively changing their tonal quality. I believe that the Tarot creates a similar imprint on the mind of the reader who familiarizes him or herself with a particular set of images. There are traditional meanings behind each, of course, but for a novice, I always suggest that you begin your Tarot journey by taking an "inventory" of the imagery supplemented by your own, devised meanings. This process requires patience and focus, but, in the end, the reward is revealed through a deeper understanding of symbolism and how to effectively read an allegorical image.

If this is in fact your first adventure into the world of the Tarot, I would suggest that you finish reading this section on usage, then put this book aside for the time being and begin the imprinting process. Consider the number of the card, the imagery displayed, and try to find similarities to stories you've read, movies you've seen, and (most importantly) events in your personal life that have similar associations. This will lead to a deeper understanding of each image than you could gain from simply reading the "little white book." You have to start somewhere, right?

Once you have spent some time (maybe a month or so) considering and studying the images, reading, playing, and having some fun with the Tarot, then and only then, do I suggest you start reading the traditional meanings and seeing how they compare to your own personal ideas. Even after you've learned these traditional meanings, I suggest you always retain the personal definitions you have created. I believe each card contains a symbolic "polyvalence" that allows for fluctuating meaning, interconnectivity and depthless analysis. The very first time you go to shuffle the deck, I would suggest looking at every card, soaking up all of the artwork. "Imprint" the deck by writing down the name of each card and a one or two word description of what that card intuitively means to you at a glance. Then, shuffle for as long as you possibly can before it becomes boring or your hands hurt or you simply cannot spare any more time. Next, place them in their box and let them sit for a day.

The next day, upon waking, give yourself a four-card reading to begin. The four cards you choose from the deck will symbolize your Spirit, Body, Mind, and Heart—in that order from left to right. Write down what you see and feel. Decide how these four cards relate to you and your present position.

When laying out the cards, place them face down. When turning the cards, flip them from right to left or from left to right as though you are opening a door. Never flip up to down or down to up because you will then reverse the card's intended meaning. (Reading "reversals" or "inversions" is something to be focused on and explored later, after you've been working with the cards for some time and have a fair grasp on their symbolism.)

That evening, look back at what you wrote down and see if you can relate it to the events of your day. If you feel the reading is accurate enough, then the bond between you and your deck is solid. If it is not, repeat the process and try again.

Shuffling before a daily reading can be done however you like. My suggestion is the standard: to shuffle the deck three times, and cut it three times. This will "cook" the deck. It's like warming it up for use. Then, you should ask the deck a preliminary question about its disposition or energy. This will set the mood for the entire reading. You can also shuffle the cards until you feel them "click." You will know it when you feel it. This is a way you can bring your intuition into the process. It is okay to ask specific questions and to flip one card at a time after the deck has been shuffled. Allow the deck up to a month to become attuned to you. Give yourself a four-card reading every day for the first month to break the deck in and familiarize yourself with the cards. Make note of repeating patterns and associations. Keeping a log of the cards that turn up each day, and writing down how you interpret what they are saying will ultimately make you a better reader.

After a month has come and gone, make note of the cards that turned up in your readings most often. This may be your Tarot's way of communicating to you what it has seen in you all along. Now that your deck is broken in, use it as you will.

SPREADS

The Four-Card Spread

There are several different spreads that you can use when laying out the cards for a reading. The four-card daily reading I mentioned previously is as simple as placing four cards side by side and reading them from left to right as being representative of your:

1=spirit, 2=body, 3=mind and 4=heart

The Question Spread

The following spread is one I have designed specifically for the *Didactic Tarot*. I call it the "Question Spread."

Ask a specific question and the cards you turn will represent…

1= The matter at hand.
2= What you intuitively know about this matter.
3= What you want (to hear/ believe) about this matter.
4= What you fear (interference) in relation to this matter.
5= One possible outcome if you continue on this path.
6= Another possible outcome if you veer from this path.
7= Advice on the matter at hand.

Of course, the positions and meanings can be adapted to your intuitive translation and more cards can be added beside any position to further clarify its meaning.

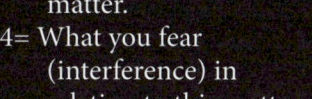

Celtic Cross Spread

My take on the standard "Celtic Cross" spread, known to most anyone who has ever picked up a Tarot deck, is outlined below.

1= The current issue.
2= The root cause of this issue (to be placed across the first card).
3= The crown you wear. This can either take the form of a radiant energy that defines and exposes your highest potential or a dark cloud that hovers over you and clouds your judgment—depending upon how you interpret the card.
4= The modus operandi. This position indicates a special ability that is innate and that you may not recognize about yourself. This is what you have to work with. I often refer to this as your "superpower!"
5= Your recent past.
6= The near future.

The second half of the reading works as a type of analysis of your position. It is a way of stepping outside of your self in order to gain some insight.

7= Attitude. This reveals how your attitude towards the current situation is affecting your ability to see the bigger picture. It is the position of clarification.
8= Environment. This is the way in which outside influences are affecting you, whether they are people, places or situations.
9= Hopes and Fears. Surprisingly, these two, diametrically opposed ideas are separated by a very, fine line. This position helps you to admit something to yourself.
10= Final outcome. This position is one of possibilities.

I never call a reading "finished" until I am satisfied by either a Higher Arcana card, a Court card or an Ace. Continue turning cards over, beside the tenth, (or the seventh in the case of the Question Spread) until one of these turns up and then read all of the cards in sequence to create a narrative of the possible future.

Some Additional Ideas to Add to Your Reading

- If the first card you turn is a Court card, it most likely represents you or someone else you know. It is the embodiment of a specific personality.
- If the first card you turn is a Higher Arcana card, it represents an important stage of life or a turning point that you are currently involved in and hence it embodies you.
- If the first card you turn is a number or Diffusion card, it represents a specific problem or something that is currently happening that needs to be addressed.

Look for patterns. If you see a lot of the same suit, say for example, the suit of Wands, then the issue is primarily a spiritual one and thus that is the aspect of life that is most in focus and having the strongest effect on you. If you see a lot of the same numbers repeating, then consider the symbolic value of that number and how it is apparent in your life. Perhaps if you see a lot of threes, you will then realize that there are three major sources of effect. You could live with two other people, be working a job while going to school and raising a child, or be dealing with three creative projects. If there are a lot of Court cards, you might realize that your social life is booming and that each of these individuals is having a distinctly different effect on you. An excessive amount of Higher Arcana cards might portend the intensity of an ever-changing situation as well as underscoring the importance of your choices in such a tumultuous time.

I have changed the names of the courtly order from Kings, Queens, Knights and Pages to Masters, Keepers, Bearers and Acolytes, (Masters control, Keepers contain, Bearers deliver and Acolytes serve), as I felt these words were more descriptive of their purposes. I have also taken the liberty of switching the astrological equivalents of the Kings and Queens. Traditionally, (although not exclusively for I have seen several variations) the "fixed" signs (Leo, Taurus, Aquarius and Scorpio) are the Kings and the "cardinal" or "hinge" signs between seasons (Aries, Capricorn, Libra and Cancer) are the Queens. I have reversed these because, although I understand the idea (being most like the King and Queen on a chessboard, the Queen is mobile and extreme in her movements and the King is very situated and stubborn on his throne, moving only when he has to) I prefer that the "hinge signs" with the highest elemental energy levels, brimming over and ready to burst, be called the "Masters" (as this would suggest the more "active" elemental property in accordance with the Taoist, "Yang" principle) and the sign that stands ready to defend the Master by unleashing the power of the element he or she deeply embodies and keeps contained until its use is absolutely required, be the "Keeper" (this is accordance with the more "passive" Taoist, "Yin" principle). This also helps to balance out the generally patriarchal hierarchy. It's all relative, really. As long as all of the signs are represented, the reader can assign them to their more traditional positions if need be.

In concluding this section, I offer this: Because the Tarot is meant to be somewhat enigmatic, the imagery has to walk a fine line between the celebration of its secrets and an exposition of its truths. In order to interpret this kind of art effectively, one must learn not only about the traditional ideas associated with each card but also, seek out the transcendental meanings behind each icon. This can only be achieved through repeated interaction with the Tarot on a divinatory, and thereby, interpretive level. One must learn how to use the Tarot and relate its messages to themselves and their individual, day-to-day experiences in order to fully grasp the flexible as well as the essential meanings. Tarot is an art form all its own. The imagery is unfathomably deep—like a passageway into the collective unconscious, into the dreams we write off as metaphysical contractions and a release of excess stimuli. It's important that we recognize the power an image can have, especially if it is conveying a universal idea. Learning to understand the symbols of the Tarot is much like learning your own dream language; it is a method for carrying on a conversation with your own as well as another's subconscious.

The best rule to follow is this: There are no rules. Find your own path and use the Tarot as you see fit. Enjoy it and learn from it, for it exists to teach, to reveal, to forewarn and ultimately for your pleasure and fulfillment.

BIBLIOGRAPHY

Bullfinch, Thomas. *Bullfinch's Mythology.* Modern Library, August 11th, 1996.
Campbell, Joseph. *The Inner Reaches of Outer Space: Metaphor as Myth and as Religion.* Novato, CA: New World Library, 2002.
Cirlot, J. E.. *A Dictionary of Symbols.* Translated by Jack Sage. New York: Philosophical Library,1962.
Crowley, Aleister. *Magick in Theory and Practice.* New York: Castle, 1960.
Drane, John. Ross Clifford. Philip Johnson. *Beyond Prediction: the Tarot and Your Spirituality.* United Kingdom; Lion. September 1st, 2001.
Guerber, H. *Myths of the Norsemen.* New York: Barnes & Noble, 2006.
Hunsicker, Robert C. *Roger Hane: Art, Times and Tragedy.* Coral Gables, Florida. Vanguard Productions 2009.
Hutton, Ronald. *The Triumph of the Moon: a History of Modern Pagan Witchcraft.* Oxford: Oxford UP, 1999.
Jaynes, Julian. *The Origin of Consciousness in the Breakdown of the Bicameral Mind.* Boston: Houghton Mifflin, 1990.
Jung, C. G. *Psyche and Symbol; a Selection from the Writings of C.G. Jung.* Garden City, NY: Doubleday, 1958.
Kandinsky, Wassily, and Michael Sadleir. *The Art of Spiritual Harmony.* S.l.: Stevenson, 2008.
Katz, Marcus. Goodwin, Tali. *Tarot Flip.* Forge Press, 2010.
Levitt, Susan. *Introduction to Tarot.* Stamford, CT: U.S. Games, 2003.
Moore, Alan. J. H. Williams III. Mick Grayk. *Promethea.* La Jolla, California, America's Best Comics 2000-2005.
Place, Robert M. *The Tarot: History, Symbolism, and Divination.* New York: The Penguin Group, 2005.
Pollack, Rachel. *78 Degrees of Wisdom.* London: Thorsons: HarperCollins, 1997.
Rosenberg, David. *Dreams of Being Eaten Alive: the Literary Core of the Kabbalah.* NewYork: Harmony, 2000.
Walker, Brian Browne. *The I Ching, Or, Book of Changes: a Guide to Life's Turning Points.* New York: St. Martin's, 1992.
Zimmer, Heinrich. *The King and the Corpse: Tales of the Soul's Conquest of Evil.* Edited by Joseph Campbell. Princeton, New Jersey: Princeton University Press, 1975.